Berlin

Front cover: the roof of the
Sony Center

Below: the Quadriga atop the
Brandenburger Tor

TOP 10 ATTRACTIONS

Sony Center • A futuristic entertainment complex at the heart of the renewed Potsdamer Platz *(page 47)*

Gendarmenmarkt • A grand square dominated by twin cathedrals *(page 55)*

Schlossbrücke • With its fine sculptures, it is Berlin's most beautiful bridge *(page 59)*

The Reichstag • Gaze from the top of this transparent parliament building *(page 38)*

Brandenburg Gate • The enduring symbol of Berlin *(page 51)*

The Pergamonmuseum • See awe-inspiring wonders of the ancient world *(page 60)*

Sanssouci • Stroll around the elegant palaces and gardens *(page 78)*

Neue Nationalgalerie • Explore this world-famous collection of 20th-century art *(page 45)*

Schloss Charlottenburg • A baroque and rococo masterpiece *(page 67)*

Jewish Museum • Where a tragic history is told *(page 54)*

CONTENTS

37

71

28

DEM DEUTSCHEN VOLKE

62

41

98

INTRODUCTION

There can be few cities more evocative of modern European history than Berlin. Almost everywhere you look, you are reminded of the dramatic events of the 20th century, for Berlin is a city which publicly acknowledges its past – good and bad – through museums, memorials, and the preservation of historically significant buildings. At times, this can feel almost overwhelmingly poignant, yet the vigour with which Berliners are embracing the future, and their determination to move forward positively while showing due respect for the suffering of the past, is immensely inspiring. A visit to this bustling, sophisticated city, which has borne witness to such extremes of human emotion, is an experience lovers of history and travel alike will not soon forget.

Since it first became Germany's capital, Berlin has excited pride for its strength, admiration for its culture, hatred as the centre of Hitler's tyranny, compassion as a bastion of post-war freedom, and fear as a focus of Cold War conflict. More than any other European capital, Berlin symbolises the immense changes wrought over the last century in Western and Eastern Europe.

For each emotion that the name Berlin evokes, the city has appropriate symbols. The noble Schloss Charlottenburg and the monuments on Unter den Linden honour the formidable Prussian past, while the Brandenburg Gate proclaims the city's regained unity. The Reichstag recalls united Germany's return to parliamentary democracy, while the gigantic Olympic Stadium expresses only too well the bombast of Hitler's dictatorship. The chaos and destruction he wreaked find their deliberate reminder in the bombed-out shell of the

Striking modern architecture at Potsdamer Platz

Kaiser Wilhelm Memorial Church, while the atrocities of the Holocaust are represented by innumerable memorials big and small, and the determination of the Jewish community to forge a stronger identity is symbolised in the restored magnificence of the Neue Synagogue.

Relics of the Old Divide

The eastern districts of the city – Mitte, Pankow, Friedrichshain and Prenzlauer Berg – essentially form the old densely populated centre whose tenements (disparagingly referred to as *Mietskasernen*, literally meaning 'rental barracks') inspired the 1920s proletarian theatre of Erwin Piscator and Bertolt Brecht. When Berlin was divided up at the end of World War II, it was appropriate that the Soviet sector devoted to the Communist experiment should take in a large number of the working-class areas, while West Berlin had at its centre the eminently bourgeois neighbourhood of Charlottenburg.

Ostalgie

As the film *Goodbye Lenin!* (2003) illustrates, there are some East Germans for whom reunification must have proved simply too much of a shock. Others may have accepted the passing of the GDR, but still look back wistfully on an era which had much good, despite the Communist dictatorship. In their nostalgia for the east (hence the term *Ostalgie*) people hanker for old certainties like jobs for life and workplace kindergartens. Basic items such as food and household products from the GDR are also high on the list. *Ostprodukte* are back in, in Berlin, just like icons that never even left, such as those red-and-green stop/go men, the *Ampelmännchen*, and that most enduring of children's TV characters, the *Sandmännchen*.

However, a rather different view of the GDR is presented in the book *Stasiland* by Anna Funder and the film *The Lives of Others* (2006), both of which examine the impact of state intrusion on personal life.

With reunification, two sets of people psychologically attuned to different economic and social systems were suddenly thrust together, and hitherto unforeseen problems emerged. As tens of thousands of East Germans came to settle in the West, entitling them to 'adjustment' money, housing subsidies and job retraining from the Bonn government, the financial burden of reunification now began to trouble West Germans, while a small minority of disgruntled West Berliners even began to wish that the Wall had never been knocked down.

Friedrichstraße S-Bahn Station

For the inhabitants of East Berlin, too, the merger with the West was less than idyllic. The sudden impact of the West's free-market economic system was in some cases disastrous, with people losing such previously enjoyed benefits as controlled rents and job security. It is taking a long time, plus an enormous ongoing investment, for, in former West German Chancellor Willy Brandt's immortal words, 'what belongs together to grow together'.

Reconstruction and Renewal

The collapse of the Wall and the integration of two independent cities led to a wealth and diversity of culture. With no fewer than three opera houses, three major symphony orchestras and two national art galleries, Berlin is justifiably proud of its renewed artistic vigour. The Kulturforum in the Tiergarten has been expanded, the magnificent Museumsinsel in the middle of the River Spree is being restored, and major new museums such as the Jüdisches Museum have opened their doors. Western Berlin's Schaubühne, along with the Berliner Ensemble, Volksbühne and Deutsches Theater from the East, now make up one of the world's most formidable theatre establishments promoting both classical tradition and the avant-garde. With the Berlin Film Festival as its flagship, cinema is resuming the excitement of its great creative period in the 1920s, a time commemorated in the exciting Film Museum Berlin *(see page 47)*.

Signs of change can be seen everywhere you go. Some cynical Berliners claim that their city has been transformed into Europe's largest building site, but the construction is yielding office, retail and living space to accommodate a grow-

The Reichstag

ing population that has been boosted by the move of government ministers and civil servants from Bonn to Berlin. Some of the new buildings are remarkably beautiful, and the city almost feels like a living art gallery. The Reichstag, once more the seat of unified Germany's parliament, is now distinguished by a vast glass dome, which represents the lack of secrecy in modern German government. Daimler-Chrysler and Sony have brought about a quite extraordinary transformation of Potsdamer Platz, and shops, offices and apartments have risen from the former Checkpoint Charlie. Gleaming new shopping malls full of designer stores have been constructed around Friedrichstraße, and old, dilapidated buildings in the east of the city have been transformed into art galleries, exclusive fashion boutiques and trendy cafés. A particular hotspot of this kind is the Scheunenviertel, the characterful area to the north of Hackescher Markt S-Bahn station.

Reflecting at the Kulturforum

Breathing Space

Despite its stone, steel and glass, Berlin is the greenest metropolis in Europe, with almost 40 percent of its area covered by lakes and rivers, parkland and woods. Besides the Tiergarten and the River Spree in the city centre, the southwest suburbs have the forest of the Grunewald, the River Havel and the Wannsee, while the north has the Tegel forest and lake. Small garden colonies abound, with flourishing farming communities, such as Lübars, set inside the city boundaries. To all of this, eastern Berlin adds its own Großer Müggelsee as well as the woods and parkland around Treptow and Köpenick.

There are more delightful excursions to be had beyond the city limits. Potsdam, at the other end of the Glienicke Bridge, lies within easy reach for a visit to Frederick the Great's Sanssouci Palace, with its extensive grounds; or you could go walking in the surrounding forests and parks of Charlottenhof, Petzow and Werder; try a spot of boating on the Templiner Lake; or even make a pilgrimage to the monastery of Lehnin near Brandenburg.

Young at Heart

Beyond sightseeing, the most fascinating thing about Berlin is its people. Throughout the city's turbulent history, the individualism, courage and wit of Berliners has elicited the admiration of the watching world. A preconceived notion of Germans as a whole, but Prussians in particular, has often presented them as a cool and unfeeling people. However, such notions are quickly dispelled by the warmth and good humour that is exhibited by many of the city's people.

Younger Berlin's so-called 'alternative scene' has revived the city's 1920s reputation of lively and wildly independent-minded creativity, sometimes foundering in disillusioned nihilism in its strongholds, the working-class districts of Neukölln and Kreuzberg. Also to be found in these districts is Berlin's large community of immigrants, originally called *Gastarbeiter* ('guest workers'), most of them from Turkey, who add considerable colour and flavour to the city's social and gastronomic life.

This sprawling, invigorating metropolis attracts more than 7 million visitors a year, none of whom can help but feel a mixture of privilege and awe at witnessing such an exciting new city in the making.

A BRIEF HISTORY

The German capital became a municipality during the 1200s, ironically as a divided city. In those days the two rival halves were in no rush to unite. The fishermen of Cölln, whose name survives in the modern borough of Neukölln, lived on an island in the River Spree. The townships that comprise the modern Mitte district grew up around market places over which the people's churches, the Nikolaikirche and Marienkirche, still tower today. With the fortress of Burg Köpenick providing a common defence to the south, Cölln and Berlin formed a trade centre between Magdeburg and Poznan.

The hub of Old Berlin around the Nikolaikirche

In a region once inhabited by Slavonic tribespeople, the population of the city was overwhelmingly German by the 13th century, comprising of enterprising merchants hailing from the northern Rhineland, Westphalia and Lower Saxony, with late-comers from Thuringia and the Harz. Berlin and Cölln came together in 1307 in order to lead the Brandenburg region's defences and defeat the robber barons who were terrorising merchants and local peasants.

The easy life

Apparently living was easy in the 15th century, as historian Trithemius noted: 'Life here consists of nothing but eating and drinking.'

The prosperous city joined the Hanseatic League, trading in rye, wool and oak timber and providing an entrepôt for skins and furs from eastern Europe.

Berlin continued as a virtually autonomous outpost of the German empire until 1448, when Brandenburg's Kurfürst (Prince Elector) Friedrich II took over control of the city after crushing the citizens' violent resistance, the so-called *Berliner Unwillen*. He was a member of the Hohenzollern dynasty that was to hold sway here for over 450 years.

The independent spirit of the Berliners was felt during the Reformation in the 16th century. The people were tired of paying the tribute exacted by the Catholic Church. In 1539, at a time when citizens of the other German principalities had to observe the religion of their prince, Berliners were successful in pressuring Prince Elector Joachim II to accept the Protestant creed as preached by Martin Luther.

Like the rest of Germany, the city was devastated by the Thirty Years' War (1618–48). Its Brandenburg rulers tried to befriend both the Protestant and Catholic armies but made enemies of both, leaving unfortified Berlin to pay the price.

Prussia – and Napoleon

With his ambition of uniting the states of Brandenburg and Prussia, it was the Great Elector Friedrich Wilhelm (1640–88) who prepared Berlin to become a strong capital, and fortified it as a garrison town. The first newcomers were 50 wealthy Jewish families who had been expelled from Vienna in 1671. Then 14 years later 5,600 Huguenot Protestants arrived after being driven out of France by the revocation of the Edict of Nantes. At a time when France was considered the cultural master of Europe, these sophisticated merchants and highly skilled craftsmen – among them jewellers, tailors, chefs and restaurant-owners – brought a new refinement to the town.

This was further enhanced by the Great Elector's son who, in 1701, crowned himself in Königsberg (now Kaliningrad) King Friedrich *in* (not *of*) Prussia. Prompted by Sophie Charlotte, his wife, the king founded academies for the arts and sciences in Berlin. Baroque master Andreas Schlüter *(see page 58)* was commissioned to redesign the royal palace. This was knocked down in 1950 to make way for East Germany's Palast der Republik. Sophie Charlotte's residence, however, the grand Schloss Charlottenburg, has been restored as a model of the era's elegance.

Friedrich Wilhelm I (1713–1740) despised the baroque glitter of his parents' court, and subjected the previously easy-going Berliners to a frugal, rigid concept of *Preussentum* (Prussianness), that is, unquestioning obedience to the ruler and his administrators, and sharply defined class distinctions, affirming the supremacy of the aristocracy, officer class and soldiers over civilians in general. An English cousin referred to Friedrich Wilhelm I as 'my brother the Sergeant', and the nickname

Schloss Charlottenburg

stuck. The Soldier King spent his life in uniform and his courtiers followed suit. He had two obsessions: corporal punishment for the troops and washing his hands wherever he went. Irascible and deeply religious, he was simple in his personal tastes, finding greatest pleasure in strictly male company over a pipe and a tankard of beer – wine struck him as too expensive.

Friedrich der Große (Frederick the Great, 1740–86), King *of* (not just *in*) Prussia, took his realm to the forefront of European politics and had little time for Berlin. He concentrated on turning his beloved Potsdam into a mini-Versailles, where French was spoken and Voltaire became his official philosopher-in-residence. He rarely appeared in Berlin except to garner public support – and taxes – after his return from costly wars with the Silesians, Russians and Austrians. He did, nevertheless, leave the German capital an enduring legacy with the monumental Forum Fridericianum laid out on Unter den Linden by his architect von Knobelsdorff.

The armies of Frederick's successors proved to be no match for Napoleon's Grande Armée, however, and as the French advanced through eastern Germany in 1806, Berlin's bureaucracy, court and bourgeoisie fled to the country. No troops were left to defend the city from its invaders, and

All The King's Cabbages

When Friedrich Wilhelm I came to the throne, a wag's graffiti on the palace wall pinpointed the costs of his parents' extravagance: 'This castle is for rent and the royal residence of Berlin for sale.' To pay off the debts, he cut court officials' salaries from 250,000 silver thalers to 50,000, sold the opulent coronation robes, melted down the palace silver, and tore the flowers out of the Schloss Charlottenburg Park and replaced them with a far more practical crop: cabbages.

Napoleon's march through the Brandenburg Gate into Berlin kindled a new flame of German patriotism.

Capital of Germany

Defying the two years of French occupation, philosopher Johann Gottlieb Fichte exhorted the German people to assume their rightful destiny as a nation. Drummers were ordered to drown out his fiery speeches at the Royal Academy.

Frederick the Great

One of the uniting forces for the nationalist movement after the defeat of Napoleon were the *Lesecafés* (reading cafés) such as Spargnapani and Kranzler. They were a rendezvous for the intelligentsia who met to read foreign and provincial newspapers and glean information withheld in the heavily censored Berlin press.

Meanwhile, the accelerating industrial revolution had produced a new Berlin proletariat of 50,000 workers. In the wake of the 1848 revolts in Paris and Vienna, demonstrations which were held to protest working and living conditions in Berlin were crushed by the Prussian cavalry, leaving 230 dead. The king made small concessions, paying lip service to the demand for press freedom. A year later, police controls had been tightened, press censorship resumed, and democratic meetings swarmed with government spies.

Prussia's success during the Franco-Prussian War (1870–71) placed it at the head of a new united Germany. Under Kaiser Wilhelm I and Chancellor Bismarck, Berlin became the *Reichshauptstadt* (capital of the empire). By 1880, amid the industrial expansion of the *Gründerzeit* (founding years), the city's population soared past the million mark. Berlin boomed as the centre of Germany's engineering industry.

After its period of rapid growth, the city began to assume its place as Germany's cultural as well as political capital, with Berlin artist Max Liebermann and others challenging Munich's dominance of German painting. The Berlin Philharmonic gained international standing, attracting Tchaikovsky, Strauss and Grieg as guest composers, and in 1905, the Viennese director Max Reinhardt arrived to head the Deutsches Theater.

Among its scientists, Robert Koch won a Nobel prize for his discovery of the *Tuberculosis bacillus*, and Max Planck headed the new Kaiser Wilhelm Society for the Advancement of Science (later named the Max-Planck-Gesellschaft), with Albert Einstein as director of the physics department.

Crowds on Potsdamer Platz at the wedding of
Victoria Louise of Prussia in 1913

War and Revolution

After years of opposition on social matters, Berliners solidly supported what proved to be the Hohenzollerns' last military gasp – World War I. At the start of the hostilities in August 1914, people gathered in thousands to cheer the Kaiser at the royal palace. The enthusiasm was short-lived.

Privations at home and the horrendous loss of life on the front turned popular feeling against the war. In 1916, Karl Liebknecht and Rosa Luxemburg formed the Spartacus League. Two years later, with Germany defeated, revolution broke out in Berlin. While the Social Democrats were proclaiming a new German Republic, Liebknecht took over the palace declaring the Republic socialist.

Vehemently opposed to any Soviet-style revolution, Chancellor Friedrich Ebert and his Social Democrats outmanoeuvred the Spartacists. Some 4,000 *Freikorps* (right-wing stormtroopers) were called in to smash the movement. They assassinated Liebknecht and Luxemburg on 15 January 1919. Four days later, a new National Assembly was elected and the dominant Social Democrats moved the government to the safety of Weimar to draw up the constitution of the new Republic.

Rosa's memorial

A memorial tablet by the Lichtenstein Bridge marks the spot where Rosa Luxemburg's body was thrown into the Landwehr Canal.

The use of the *Freikorps* to suppress the Spartacists was to haunt the Weimar Republic. In March 1920, the Kapp Putsch brought 5,000 of the storm-troopers into Berlin with an obscure civil servant, Wolfgang Kapp, installed as puppet chancellor. The coup lasted only five days, but set the tone for Germany's fragile experiment in parliamentary democracy. The swastika displayed on the helmets of the *Freikorps* was to reappear on the armbands of Hitler's storm-troopers, crushing all democracy in 1933.

The Golden Twenties

The turbulent twenties gave Berlin a special place in the world's popular imagination. In 1920, the incorporation of eight townships and some 60 suburban communities into the metropolis effectively doubled Berlin's population overnight to four million. Before democracy was extinguished in 1933, the city led a charmed life of exciting creativity that left its mark on the whole of European culture. Defeat in World War I had shattered the rigid certainties of Berlin's 'Prussianness' and left the town open to radical adventures in social and artistic expression almost unimaginable in the older cultural capitals of Vienna, London and Paris.

Artists of the avant-garde intellectual movement known as Dada called for state prayers to be replaced by simultaneous poetry and regularisation of sexual intercourse via a Central Dada Sex Office. Many years before the New York 'happenings' of the 1960s, Berlin Dadaists were organising races between a sewing machine and a typewriter, with writer Walter Mehring and artist Georg Grosz as jockeys. In the meantime, nightclubs on Tauentzienstraße provided a combination of political satire and striptease, accompanied by copious amounts of alcohol, cocaine and sexual licence. The paintings of Otto

Film Greats

Berlin showed its sense of the times with its mastery of film, the 20th-century art form. Fritz Lang, F.W. Murnau, G.W. Pabst and Ernst Lubitsch were the leading directors of their generation. While Hollywood had considered cinema to be principally an industry of mass entertainment, the Berlin film-makers added a new perception of its artistic possibilities with M, The Cabinet of Dr Caligari, Lulu and Nosferatu. After seeing Fritz Lang's premonitory fable of human regimentation, Metropolis, Hitler wanted the master of the dark spectacle to make publicity films for him.

Dix, Georg Grosz and Max Beckmann were brutally realist, and the dissonance of the times was aptly captured by the atonal music composed by Arnold Schönberg and his pupil Alban Berg.

The conservative establishment winced when the Prussian Writers' Academy chose as its president Heinrich Mann, the elder brother of Thomas Mann, a violent critic of the bourgeoisie and a Communist Party supporter. His best-known novel, *Professor Unrat*, inspired Josef von Sternberg's *The Blue Angel*, the film that revealed the vocal talents of Marlene Dietrich.

A show in the 1920s

Berlin was going through a wild time, but the Versailles peace treaty had laid heavy burdens on the nation. At the start of the twenties, inflation had made little more than nonsense of the German currency, and political assassinations became routine. The most significant of the victims was foreign minister Walther Rathenau, an enlightened democrat and Jew who was killed near the Grunewald forest. It was also the time of vicious street battles between Communists and Nazis, exploiting the social disruptions of inflation and unemployment that were impossible to ignore.

The Third Reich

Communist hostility towards the Social Democrats split the opposition to the Nazis. Hitler became Chancellor on 30 January 1933. Only a month later, on 27 February, the Reichstag went up in flames. Hitler used the fire as a pretext to elim-

Nazi torchlit parade, 1933

inate Communist and all left-wing opposition from German political life. The Nazi reign of terror had begun.

Flames were the leitmotiv of the Third Reich in Berlin. On 10 May 1933, a procession brought thousands of students along Unter den Linden to the square before Humboldt University. They carried books, not to a lecture but to a bonfire on which were burned the works of Thomas Mann, Heinrich Mann, Stefan Zweig, Albert Einstein and Sigmund Freud, as well as Proust, Zola, Gide, H.G. Wells and Jack London. In 1936 a flame was brought from Athens to Berlin to inaugurate the Olympic Games, an attempt at Aryan propaganda which was soundly subverted by black athlete Jesse Owens, who won four gold medals. In deference to foreign visitors, all anti-Semitic signs such as *Juden unerwünscht* (Jews not wanted) were removed from shops, hotels and cafés. As soon as the foreigners had left town, the signs went up again.

Discrimination against the Jews moved inexorably to the night of 9 November 1938, when synagogues and other Jewish-owned buildings were burned, and shops looted. This pogrom came to be called *Kristallnacht*, 'the Night of Broken Glass'. Berlin's Jewish population, which stood at 170,000 in 1933, was reduced by emigration and extermination to around 6,000 by 1945.

World War II

In the autumn of 1938, as Hitler's army was preparing its march into neighbouring Czechoslovakia, Berliners shared none of the fervour that had greeted military parades in 1914. Their disquiet was shortly to be justified. The first bombing raids came in 1940 from the British in retaliation for the air raids on London. Attacks were stepped up after the German defeat at Stalingrad in 1943, with Anglo-American 'carpet-bombing'. The worst single raid was on 6 February 1945, when bombs wiped out 4 sq km (1½ sq miles) of the city centre in one hour. Hitler spent the last days of the war in his bunker at the Reich chancellery. As Soviet troops moved in to capture the city, he killed himself with a shot through the mouth.

The war ended with unconditional German surrender on 8 May 1945. In Berlin, the population was left to pick up the pieces – literally. Women formed groups of *Trümmerfrauen* (rubble women), with 60,000 of them passing the debris of war by hand to clear the ground for rebuilding.

Division and Reunification

With the Soviet army already in place, American troops entered Berlin in 1945 on their national Independence Day, 4 July, followed by the British and French contingents. Four-power control of Berlin was agreed at Potsdam by Winston Churchill, Harry Truman and Joseph Stalin. The Soviet eastern sector covered just under half the city's area; the French, British and Americans divided the western sector between them.

The Allies soon found themselves confronted with Soviet efforts to incorporate the whole of Berlin into a Communist-controlled eastern Germany. In the 1946 municipal elections – Berlin's first free vote since 1933, and its last until 1990 – the Social Democrats won a crushing victory over the Communists, prompting the Soviets to tighten their grip on the eastern sector. Unhappy that West Berlin's capitalist presence in

Airlift in progress

the middle of East Germany was having a subversive influence on the Communist experiment, the Soviets and their East German allies began to restrict traffic from West Germany. In June 1948, all road, rail and waterway routes to West Berlin were sealed off. The Western Allies countered the blockade by airlifting into Berlin between 4,000 and 8,000 tons of food and other vital supplies every day for 11 months. The blockade ended in May 1949, and West Berlin became a *Land* linked administratively with the new Federal Republic of Germany (which had Bonn as its capital). East Berlin was made capital of the fledgling German Democratic Republic (GDR).

Discontent with living conditions in East Berlin first erupted into open revolt on 17 June 1953. Striking workers marched down Stalinallee (later renamed Karl-Marx-Allee) to demonstrate against the government of Walter Ulbricht. They were protesting against the state demands for increased productivity while their standard of living continued to compare poorly with that of West Berlin. The revolt was crushed by Soviet tanks.

By the end of the 1950s, over 3 million citizens had fled East Germany in search of a better life, over half of them through Berlin. The authorities decided to put a stop to the haemorrhage. In the early hours of 13 August 1961, the East Germans began to erect the wall that would separate East and West Berlin and change the lives of several million people for nearly 30 years. Masterminded by Ulbricht and Erich Honecker, the Berlin Wall grew from an improvised barbed-wire fence into a massive barrier close to 4m (13ft) high, topped by concrete tubing. Behind it, protected by an electrified fence, stretched a strip of sand 150m (160yds) wide – a no-man's land equipped with watch-towers, patrol dogs and searchlights. The most poignant stretch was in the district of Wedding, where Bernauerstraße ran one side in the east, the other in the west. After the border was closed in August 1961, people jumped to freedom from windows until workmen bricked them up.

For the Western Alliance, the Wall made West Berlin an even more powerful symbol of freedom. On his visit in 1963, US President John F. Kennedy dramatically underlined the Western Allies' commitment to the city with his famous proclamation: '*Ich bin ein Berliner.*'

Erich Honecker's regime won international diplomatic recognition for East Berlin as its capital and, with gleaming hotels and skyscrapers, tried to give it a lustre to rival West Berlin. Beneath the surface, however, the drabness of daily life and lack of personal freedom undermined any chance of popular support.

Break for freedom

Civilian escapes by tunnel, cars with hidden compartments, and other subterfuges, including by hot-air balloon, became as much a part of the Cold War legend as break-outs by prisoners of war in World War II.

The final push which led to the collapse of the Berlin Wall came when an ecological campaign in Leipzig against nuclear weapons and industrial pollution grew into nationwide pressure for democratic freedom. In 1989, with thousands of East Germans fleeing to the West via Hungary, Czechoslovakia and Poland, the country was swept up in the wave of eastern European revolutions unleashed by the reforms of Soviet leader Mikhail Gorbachev. His visit to East Berlin in October 1989 for the 40th anniversary of the GDR left it clear that Soviet troops would no longer shore up its regime. The Berlin Wall was opened on 9 November 1989, and at midnight on 3 October 1990, a huge black, red and gold national flag was hoisted at the Reichstag. East and West Berlin were united once more.

The City Today

With a population of almost three and a half million, re-united Berlin was far and away Germany's largest city and was quickly declared the national capital again. On 20 June 1991, the city's role at the hub of German life was assured when the Bundestag voted by a slim majority to restore Berlin as the seat of government. In May 1999 a federal President was elected at the Reichstag and, in August that year, government business was finally moved from Bonn to Berlin.

Berlin has continued its transformation in the early years of the 21st century. The new government quarter is now ready and new foreign embassies have been erected and old ones refurbished. Restoration of historic buildings has also proceeded apace, and the realisation of major new schemes such as at Potsdamer Platz has made Berlin a showcase for modern urban design. The latest addition to the architectural attractions is the giant Hauptbahnhof (Central Station), an attractive glass palace close to the Kanzleramt (Federal Chancellery). In 2006 the city hosted a number of matches in the football World Cup, including the final, in the recently modernised Olympic Stadium.

Historical Landmarks

Beginnings

1237–44 First record of Cölln and Berlin.

1307 The two townships are consolidated as one city.

1486 Residence of the Elector of Brandenburg.

Reformation

1539 Berliners force Elector Joachim II to turn Protestant.

1618–48 Thirty Years' War and plague halve population to barely 5,000.

1696–1700 Arts and science academies founded.

Rise of Prussia

1740–86 Frederick the Great ascends the throne.

1791 Brandenburg Gate completed.

1806–8 Napoleon occupies Berlin.

1848 Democratic revolt crushed.

Capital of Germany

1871 Bismarck imposes Berlin as capital of Germany.

1918 November Revolution; new Republic at the Reichstag.

1933 Hitler imposes dictatorship after Reichstag fire.

1936 Berlin hosts XI Olympic Games.

1938 9 November: Kristallnacht pogrom.

1939–45 World War II cuts population in half.

Division and Unification

1945 Berlin is divided and controlled by the Four Powers (France, the Soviet Union, the usa and Great Britain).

1953 17 June: Soviet tanks crush East Berlin uprising.

1961 Construction of the Berlin Wall.

1989 East German regime toppled; Berlin Wall opened.

1990 Reunited Berlin elects its first unified parliament in over 40 years.

1991 Berlin again becomes the seat of government.

1999 The Bundestag commences business at the Reichstag.

2001 The city's 23 boroughs are amalgamated into 12 new ones.

2006 Football World Cup held in Germany.

2007 Berlin celebrates the 50th anniversary of the Treaty of Rome.

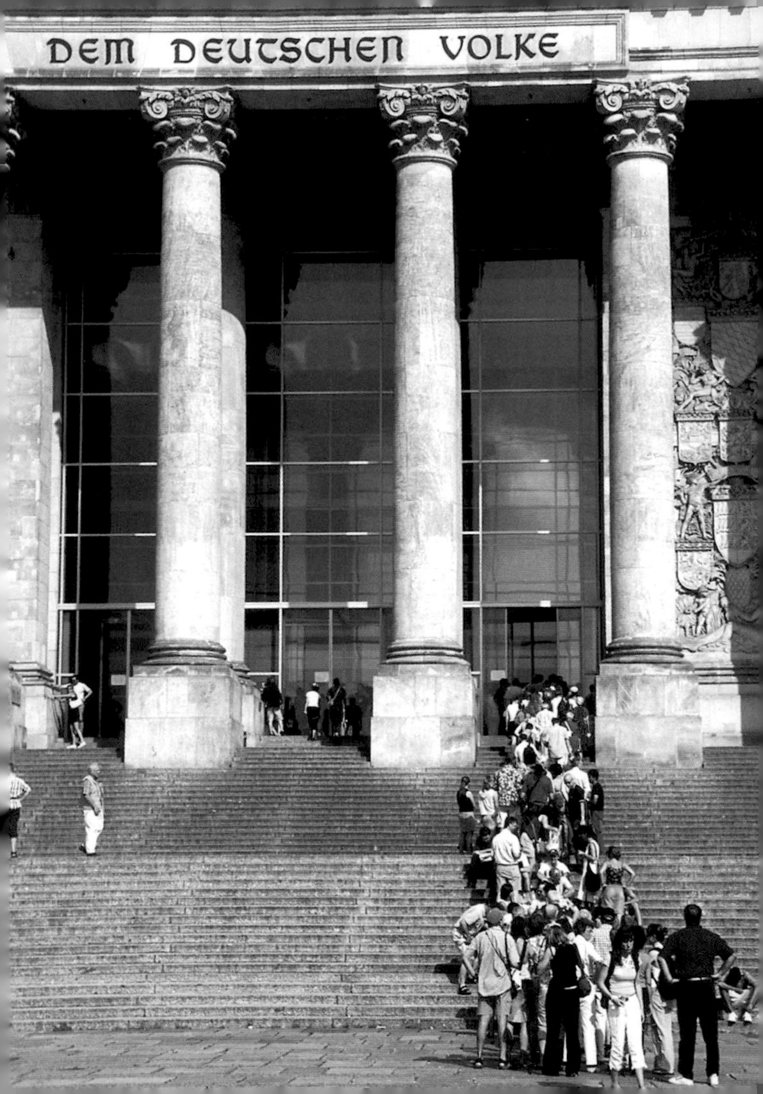
DEM DEUTSCHEN VOLKE

WHERE TO GO

You'll need to plan carefully for a thorough exploration of Berlin – with a total area of 880 sq km (340 sq miles) it is more than eight times the size of Paris. Since the reorganisation of the municipal transport system, virtually the whole of the city is accessible via underground (U-Bahn), district (S-Bahn) railways, bus or tram. You should have no difficulty in reaching the outlying areas, including Grunewald and Potsdam, by public transport (which runs 24 hours a day). There is absolutely no need for a car in Berlin.

A good orientation exercise is to start with an organised sightseeing tour. Many bus tours, for instance, depart from the eastern end of the Kurfürstendamm. Alternatively, cruises on the Landwehrkanal or Spree and Havel rivers offer a more leisurely way of taking in areas of eastern and western Berlin that are not normally covered by the tour buses.

This guide takes in the sights of Central Berlin from west to east, starting at the

Taking the S-Bahn

A good initial way of getting the measure of Berlin is to take the S-Bahn around the central area, from Zoologischer Garten to Alexanderplatz. From the elevated track you get impressive views of some major landmarks, including the Reichstag.

Kurfürstendamm, then onto the Tiergarten Area, and through the Brandenburg Gate to Unter Den Linden. In the west, a **BERLIN infostore** can be found at the Budapester Straße side of the Europa-Center and is open every day; the helpful staff will assist you with maps, leaflets and other useful information.

Queuing to get into the Reichstag *(see page 38)*

Kurfürstendamm U-Bahn station

AROUND THE KURFÜRSTENDAMM

Western Berlin's main thoroughfare, literally 'Prince Elector's Embankment', is known to Berliners as the **Ku'damm**.
It extends for 3.5km (about 2 miles) through the western
part of the city centre, forming a triangular area enclosed
by Lietzenburger Straße, Hardenbergstraße, Leibnizstraße
and Tauentzienstraße. Here you'll find a vast array of
shops, cafés, restaurants, theatres, cinemas and art galleries, as well as no-frills fast-food stands and the inevitable
souvenir sellers.

Impressed by the prolongation of the Champs-Elysées in
Paris to the Bois de Boulogne, Bismarck wanted to extend
the Ku'damm out as far as the Grunewald forest. However,
such pretentions were never realised, and finally the avenue
linked Kaiser Wilhelm Memorial Church to nothing grander
than the Halensee railway station.

The avenue lost almost all the Jugendstil architecture of its Wilhelminian heyday during World War II, and only a few vestiges survive. Otherwise the street is resolutely modern – gleaming glass, steel and an occasional touch of marble – but still a magnet for fashionable shopping.

Kranzler Eck

Like so much of the city, this area is in a constant state of re-development. The **Kranzler Eck** (Kranzler Corner), where the city's most stylish citizens once sat for coffee and cakes, has been transformed by the addition of a stunning 16-storey glass skyscraper, designed by Helmut Jahn of Chicago and completed in 2002. As well as offices, the new City Quartier has shops and restaurants. The **Café Kranzler** is still there, but it no longer looks quite as dominant as it once did.

Off the Ku'damm at Fasanenstraße 79 you will find the **Jüdisches Gemeindezentrum** (Jewish Community Centre). Framing the entrance is the domed portal from the synagogue which was burned during the fateful *Kristallnacht* ('Night of Broken Glass') of 1938 *(see page 22)*. The modern building serves as a cultural centre for the 12,000 Jews still living in Berlin today – in 1933 they numbered some 170,000.

At Fasanenstraße 24 stands the intimate **Käthe-Kollwitz Museum** (open Wed–Mon 11am–6pm). On display is a comprehensive collection of sketches, drawings and sculptures by the artist Käthe Kollwitz (1867–1945), whose work resounds with compassion as she makes appeals on

Helmut Jahn's glass tower at Kranzler Eck

Literaturhaus

Next door to the Käthe-Kollwitz Museum is the Literaturhaus, where readings, seminars and discussions are held. The villa is surrounded by a delightful garden, and there's a pleasant café, the Café Wintergarten.

behalf of the working poor, the suffering and the sick.

It's worth exploring some of the other side streets off the Ku'damm. As well as Fasanenstraße, you will discover many other elegant tree-lined boulevards studded with beautiful, balconied villas, antiques shops, art galleries and exclusive designer boutiques. A little to the north, **Savignyplatz** provides a focus for first-class art and architecture bookshops and art galleries, located in the arches beneath the overhead S-Bahn railway line. Here you will find an abundance of literary cafés, bistros and bars, with plenty of outside seating.

Breitscheidplatz

To the east of the Kranzler Eck, the Ku'damm leads through to **Breitscheidplatz**, a big pedestrianised area at the base of the Europa-Center and a busy gathering place for shoppers and sightseers during the day. In the centre of the square is Joachim Schmettau's granite **Weltkugelbrunnen** (or Fountain of the World), which locals have gaily christened the Wasserklops ('aquatic meatball').

Soaring above it is an enduringly powerful symbol of the city, the **Kaiser-Wilhelm-Gedächtniskirche** (Kaiser-Wilhelm Memorial Church). The 1943 bombing, combined with artillery fire at the end of the war, left the tower with the broken stump of its spire – 63m (206ft) compared with its original 113m (370ft) – as a monumental ruin recalling the city's destruction. Flanking it, a modern octagonal church to the east and a chapel and hexagonal tower to the west represent the city's post-war rebirth. Stained glass made in Chartres

Christ the King mosaic in the Kaiser-Wilhelm Memorial Church

and set in walls of moulded concrete casts a mysterious bluish glow over the Ku'damm at night.

Built between 1891 and 1895 to honour Wilhelm I, the remains of this neo-Romanesque church constitute a memorial hall to celebrate the Hohenzollerns' pious monarchism. A mosaic representing Christ the King is set above friezes and reliefs of Prussian monarchs from Friedrich I (1415–40) to the last crown prince, Friedrich Wilhelm. On one wall, Wilhelm I confers with Chancellor Bismarck and Field Marshals Moltke and Roon. With their taste for irreverent nicknames, Berliners have deflated the monuments' imperial or pacifist intentions by dubbing the original church the 'broken tooth' and the two main additions the 'lipstick' and 'powder compact'.

Beyond the church is the enormous **Europa-Center**, between Tauentzienstraße and Budapester Straße. The centre was built in the 1960s and houses scores of shops, restaurants, a hotel and a theatre amid artificial ponds and water-falls. On top the Europa-Center, close to the Mercedes star, is the 'Heliport', where visitors can experience a video simulation of an adventurous flight over Berlin.

A multi-media experience in the Ku'damm Karree (Ku'damm 207–208) dramatically relates 800 years of the city's history. The frequent English-language tours relating **The Story of Berlin** (open daily 10am–8pm) include a visit to a nuclear blast-proof underground bunker.

The Zoo

Berlin sculpture, with the Europa-Center and Kaiser-Wilhelm Memorial Church

The **Zoo**, entrance on Budapester Straße (daily Apr–Sept 9am–6.30pm, Oct 9am–6pm, Nov–Feb 9am–5pm, Mar 9am–5.30pm), is the oldest zoo in Germany (1841) and has one of the most varied collections of animals in Europe. Beyond the colourful and pagoda-arched **Elefantentor** (Elephant Gate) are 35 hectares (86 acres) of parkland where you will be able to observe Indian and African elephants, giant pandas and the rare Indian single-horned rhinoceros. Originally dating from 1913, the **Zoo-Aquarium Berlin** houses numerous species of fish and reptiles, and an impressive collection of arthropods.

Tauentzienstraße

From Breidscheidplatz, follow the double-laned **Tauentzienstraße** to the east. In the pleasantly landscaped central reservation, notice the intertwined steel tubes of the *Berlin* sculpture, which was designed for the city's 750th anniversary in 1987. The two halves are tantalisingly close to each other, yet fail to touch, poignantly symbolising the once divided city.

Elephant at the Zoo

Wittenbergplatz

At the far end of Tauentzienstraße, **Wittenbergplatz** is a large, populous square and contains one of Berlin's many memorials: a stark sign outside the U-Bahn station which reminds passers-by of the Nazi concentration camps. The station itself is a beautifully restored art deco delight with lovely wooden ticket booths, period posters and a central standing clock.

More than just a department store, **KaDeWe** (Kaufhaus des Westens), located on the edge of Wittenbergplatz, has achieved the status of a monument since its foundation in 1907. The food emporium on the sixth floor is extraordinary. Here, gourmet globetrotters can perch on a bar stool and sample not only food from all over Germany but also Chinese, Japanese, Russian, French and Swiss cuisine. One floor up, the Wintergarten is a vast food court in the glass-roofed atrium where shoppers can help themselves to tasty fare. It's an ideal spot for a hearty breakfast before a day's shopping. The fashion department (on three floors) is also well worth a visit.

TIERGARTEN AREA

Despite its name, the leafy **Tiergarten** (literally 'animal garden') is not another zoo. For the Hohenzollern princes, it was a forest for hunting deer and wild boar. After Frederick the Great cut down the woods to create a formal French garden for his brother August Ferdinand, it was replanted with trees in the 19th century and transformed into a landscaped park. Following World War II the Berliners stripped away the trees again – for fuel. Everything you see here has been planted since 1950, among pleasant ponds, cafés and various monuments.

Within the park, the **Englischer Garten** was laid out by the Shropshire Horticultural Society, and forms part of the grounds of the neoclassical **Schloss Bellevue**, official residence of the German President.

Hansaviertel

On the northwest side of the Tiergarten is the **Hansaviertel**, a residential neighbourhood rebuilt by architects for the International Building Exhibition of 1957. Among the winners were Bauhaus founder Walter Gropius (Händelallee 1–9), the Brazilian Oscar Niemeyer (Altonaer Straße 4–14) and Alvar Aalto from Finland (Klopstockstraße 30). Their names are inscribed along with the locations of their projects on a map on Klopstockstraße. Nearby, at Hanseatenweg 10, the **Akademie der Künste** (Arts Academy), distinguished by the splendid Henry Moore sculpture outside, holds concerts, plays and exhibitions of avant-garde art.

Siegessäule

At the centre of the park, on the circle of the Großer Stern, the soaring **Siegessäule** (Victory Column) is an unabashed monument to Prussian militarism. It was completed in 1873, two years after the victory over the French, and also marks successes against Denmark (1864) and Austria (1866). A climb of around 285 steps takes you to the top of the 67m (220ft) column for a breathtaking view of the city from under the gilded bronze statue of Winged Victory.

During the 2006 World Cup, the Straße des 17 Juni from here to the Brandenburg Gate was the scene of the 'FIFA Fan Fest' – probably the biggest soccer party in the world.

The Siegessäule

Haus der Kulturen der Welt

On the north side of the Großer Stern are monuments honouring the architects of that first unification, the Field Marshals Moltke and Roon, and Chancellor Bismarck. Follow the River Spree to the east along Spreeweg until you reach the former **Kongreßhalle**, built by the Americans as their contribution to the 1957 International Building Exhibition. Officially renamed **Haus der Kulturen der Welt** (House of World Cultures), the striking design, with its curved concrete roof, led Berliners to dub the building the 'pregnant oyster'. In front of the building, the pond features a sculpture by Henry Moore, and is attractively illuminated at night. An austere black structure stands on the corner of Große Querallee near the Kongreßhalle. Built in 1987, the 42m- (138ft-) tall tower contains a 68-bell **carillon**, which chimes daily at noon and 6pm.

Reichstag

A few minutes' walk eastwards from the Haus der Kulturen der Welt you'll find the **Reichstag** building (S-Bahn Friedrichstraße, open daily 8am–midnight, last admission 10pm), its huge, new glass dome, with its mirrored central funnel, visible from much of the city and symbolic of a new Germany that keeps no secrets from its people. The parliamentary home of Wilhelminian and Weimar Germany displays the proud dedication *Dem deutschen Volke* (To the German People) on a neoclassical facade built in 1894 by Paul Wallot. This appeal to patriotism and democracy, set above six Corinthian columns, outlasted the burning in 1933 and the bombs of World War II, and was given renewed significance when Berlin resumed its former role as the seat of government of a unified Germany. Today, the dome, designed by Sir Norman Foster, is a major attraction for Berliners and tourists alike. They endure lengthy queues to be able to travel to the top, gazing out at the city and down into the Bundestag chamber.

The Reichstag now forms the centrepiece of what is otherwise a completely new government quarter. Among the cool modern buildings spanning the bend in the River Spree stands the new **Federal Chancellery**, nicknamed the 'Washing Machine' by irreverent locals. Adjacent to the Reichstag,

Through a glass

The Reichstag's glass dome is designed to direct natural light and ventilation into the Bundestag chamber below; at night it reflects the artificial light coming from the chamber.

the river is straddled by an impressive complex designed by Stefan Braunfels: the **Paul-Löbe-Haus** on the south bank, housing the committee rooms of the Bundestag and parliamentarians' offices, linked by a bridge to the **Marie-Elisabeth-Lüders-Haus**, which houses archive and library facilities. The largest modern complex in the Reichstag vicinity is the gigantic **Jakob-Kaiser-Haus**, behind the Reichstag itself, which is where the political parties have their headquarters and offices. It's worth taking a stroll past this, along the **promenade** which runs bet-

The promenade and memorial

ween the Reichstag and Friedrichstraße station; among the features to look out for here is a sculpture representing the Berlin Wall behind glass panelling with paragraphs of the German Constitution etched into it, and, near the Paul-Löbe-Haus, a metal memorial with white crosses on a black background, erected in honour of six East Germans killed in 1962 while attempting to flee to the West.

Hamburger Bahnhof

Easily reached from the Reichstag via one of the Spree bridges, and within easy reach of the impressive new Hauptbahnhof, along Invalidenstraße, are two of Berlin's most fascinating museums. A splendid example of early railway architecture,

Hamburger Bahnhof

the elegant old **Hamburger Bahnhof** (open Tues–Fri 10am–6pm, Sat 11am–8pm, Sun 11am–6pm) is now the Museum of Contemporary Art, a spacious setting for works by modern masters like Joseph Beuys and Andy Warhol. Another venerable building, the 100-year-old **Museum für Naturkunde** (Natural History Museum, open Tues–Fri 9.30am–5pm, Sat–Sun 10am–6pm) is one of the finest of its kind. It has some 25 million objects in its collection. The dinosaur hall, which displays the world's largest dinosaur skeleton, recently reopened after restoration.

Bauhaus Archiv

Back in the Tiergarten, south of the Siegessäule at the corner of Stülerstraße and Klingelhöferstraße, stands the elegant, modern shared complex which houses the **Embassies of the Nordic Countries** (Denmark, Finland, Norway, Sweden and Iceland). Completed in 1999, the architecture is a stunning showcase for Scandinavian design and materials.

Near the bridge over the Landwehrkanal, the stylised curves of the **Bauhaus Archiv** were designed by Walter Gropius, founder of the Bauhaus school of architecture, art and design. The **Museum für Gestaltung** here (Design Museum, open Wed–Mon 10am–5pm) documents the hugely influential achievements of the Bauhaus, the most progressive early 20th-century institution of its kind. Architects like Gropius himself, Mies van der Rohe and Marcel Breuer collaborated with artists such as Paul Klee, Vasili Kandinsky, Lyonel Feininger, Oskar Schlemmer and Laszlo Moholy-Nagy in an attempt to integrate arts, crafts and architecture into mass industrial society. On view here is a selection of the objects they created: tubular steel chairs, cups and saucers, teapots, desks, new weaves for carpets, chess pieces and children's building blocks, as well as some pioneering architectural plans and sketches.

Stauffenbergstraße

Follow the north bank of the tree-lined Landwehrkanal along the Reichpietschufer as far as Stauffenbergstraße. On the corner stands one of Berlin's most striking works of Modernist architecture, the **Gasag Building** (or Shell Haus), designed by Emil Fahrenkamp and built for Shell Oil in 1930. This was one of the first steel-framed 'high-rise' buildings in Berlin. Its

The curved lines of Emil Fahrenkamp's Gasag Building

Gedenkstätte Deutscher Widerstand

flowing curves, lightness of style and use of glass provide a stark contrast to the Nazi architecture built later in the 1930s, as seen, for example, in the Japanese Embassy on nearby Hildebrandstraße, or indeed at the next attraction. The **Gedenkstätte Deutscher Widerstand** (open Mon–Fri 9am–6pm, Thur 9am–8pm, Sat–Sun 10am–6pm) at Stauffenbergstraße 13–14 is a memorial to German resistance against the Nazi regime, located within the *Bendlerblock*, the former German military headquarters. A bronze statue depicting a young man with bound hands stands in the courtyard where Graf von Stauffenberg and other army officers (who conspired to blow up Hitler on 20 July 1944) were shot. An excellent exhibition, in the rooms of the building where the attempted coup was planned, charts the tragic course of resistance.

Follow Stauffenbergstraße to its junction with Tiergartenstraße. At the corner is the **Austrian Embassy**. Designed by Austrian architect Hans Hollein and completed in 2001, its three distinct parts rendered in turquoise, lilac and grey reflect the different functions within the building. The embassy marks the eastern gateway to the diplomatic quarter which runs along Tiergartenstraße to the left. In the other direction, Tiergartenstraße leads straight to the Kulturforum.

Kulturforum

Situated just west of Potsdamer Platz, the **Kulturforum** (S-Bahn/U-Bahn Potsdamer Platz) is a complex of concert halls and museums built on land levelled by both the plans of Albert Speer (Hitler's architect) to redesign the city and the bombs of World War II. It is clustered around the only building to survive from previous eras, the **Matthäikirche**, which was built in the neo-Romanesque style in 1846 by August Stüler and stands in dignified isolation on Matthäikirchplatz.

The quality of exhibits in the museums here is outstanding. Completed in 1998, the **Gemäldegalerie** (open Tues–Sun 10am–6pm, Thur 10am–10pm) is home to a remarkable collection of German and European paintings from the 13th to the 19th centuries. Among the works are masterpieces such as Hans Holbein's *Portrait of Georg Gisze* (1532); the rather amusing *The Fountain of Youth* (1546) by Lucas Cranach the Elder; Van Eyck's *Portrait of Giovanni Arnolfini* (1440); Van Dyck's portraits of a Genoese couple (1626); Vermeer's study, *Young Lady with a Pearl Necklace* (1644) and, among one of the largest Rembrandt collections in the world, a portrait of the artist's second wife, Hendrickje Stoffels (1659).

Adjacent to the gallery, the **Kunstgewerbemuseum** (open Tues–Fri 10am–6pm, Sat–Sun 11am–6pm) from 1985 displays a wide range of the most exquisitely executed arts and crafts, from medieval times to the present day. Among its outstanding treasures is the Welfenschatz, comprising dazzling examples of the goldsmith's

Vermeer's *Young Lady with a Pearl Necklace*, Gemäldegalerie

Early birds

With popular temporary exhibitions, the queue for the Neue Nationalgalerie can stretch right round the building. Try to get there good and early.

art from the 11th to the 15th centuries – richly bejewelled crosses, reliquaries and portable altars, presented to St Blasius Cathedral in Brunswick by successive generations of Guelph (Welf) dukes. Other prized exhibits include glazed Italian majolica and a quite bewitching collection of porcelain – Chinese, Meissen, Frankenthal, Nymphenburg, as well as Berlin's own Königliche Porzellan Manufaktur (the royal KPM).

The **Kupferstichkabinett** (Prints and Drawings Collection, open Tues–Fri 10am–6pm, Sat–Sun 11am–6pm) is one of the world's finest graphics collections, with works ranging from 14th-century illuminated manuscripts to modern woodcuts by Erich Heckel and lithographs by Willem de Kooning. Also on display are outstanding works by Dürer, Botticelli and Rembrandt.

The architect Hans Scharoun is famous for his Expressionistic free-form structures. His first design, the controversial ochre and gold **Philharmonie**, owes its tent-like shape to the demands of the concert hall's acoustics and sight-lines. The home of the Berlin Philharmonic Orchestra was designed from the inside out, from the orchestra to the walls and roof. Viewed from across Tiergartenstraße, the nearby **Musikinstrumentenmuseum** (open Tues–Fri 9am–5pm, Thur 9am–10pm, Sat–Sun 10am–5pm), also by Scharoun, is reminiscent of an open card index file. Its extensive collection of instruments from the 16th century to the present includes a 1703 Stradivarius violin, the 1810 piano of composer Carl Maria von Weber, and a 1929 New York Wurlitzer cinema organ, which comes alive in a concert given at noon every Saturday. Tours are conducted every Saturday at 11am.

The nearby **Staatsbibliothek** (State Library), Potsdamer Straße 33, was also designed by Scharoun. Despite its formidable dimensions, the library is a model of peace and harmony. A quite ingenious network of staircases leads to multi-level reading rooms and easily accessible stacks. It's one of the largest modern library buildings in Europe, and regularly holds documentary and photographic exhibitions as well as concerts.

Neue Nationalgalerie

Just south of the Matthäikirche at the corner of Potsdamer Straße, though not part of the Kulturforum, is the **Neue Nationalgalerie** (open Tues–Fri 10am–6pm, Thur 10am–10pm, Sat–Sun 11am–6pm). This square, glass-wall structure with its vast, black steel roof supported by eight massive steel columns, was designed by Bauhaus master Mies van der Rohe and completed in 1968, a year before his death. The building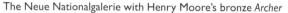

The Neue Nationalgalerie with Henry Moore's bronze *Archer*

is of characteristic elegant simplicity and considered a prime example of structural abstraction emblematic of the International Style. It stands on a raised granite platform that serves as a sculpture court for huge pieces like Henry Moore's *Archer*.

The gallery houses an outstanding collection of 20th-century painting and sculpture, the main focus being on Cubism, Expressionism, Bauhaus and Surrealism. The development of Cubism is shown through works by Picasso, Gris, Leger and Lauens, while Expressionism is represented by some notable works of Max Beckmann as well as artists from the group *Die Brücke*, with works by Kirchner (*Potsdamer Platz*, 1914), Schmidt-Rottluff and Heckel. Surrealist paintings by Max Ernst, Salvador Dalí and Joán Miró are also displayed, as are New Objectivity works by Otto Dix and George Grosz. Exponents of the Bauhaus style represented here include Kandinsky and Klee; there are also some American paintings from the 1960s and 1970s, including abstract works by Frank Stella and Ellsworth Kelly. During temporary exhibitions held over long periods several times a year, the gallery's permanent collection is not on view.

A piece of the past

A poignant contrast to the futuristic architecture and technological content of the Sony Center can be found in the elegant remains of the old Grandhotel Esplanade, now preserved behind glass walls at the entrance. Before it was almost completely destroyed during World War II, the hotel was a meeting point for the international rich and famous, including stars such as Greta Garbo and Charlie Chaplin.

Potsdamer Platz

Reduced by war and the Wall to a bleak no-man's-land, the square that was at one time the busiest in Europe has burst back into life in the most invigorating fashion. What was once a scar on the landscape, epitomising the division of the city and country, is now a thriving arts, entertainment, shopping and business centre. The impact of the towering, modern buildings, made predominantly from glass, is breathtaking. Investment from corporations such as Daimler-Chrysler and Sony has resulted in the construction of shopping malls, a theatre, casino, splendid hotels, cinemas and a film museum.

Almost 100,000 people a day come here to marvel at the striking architecture and explore the latest attractions in this ever-changing city-within-a-city. The **Sony Center** is a vibrant entertainment complex, contained within a central courtyard under a glass ceiling. Technophiles

A touch of New York or Chicago at Potsdamer Platz

can check out the latest gadgets at Sony's first European department store, while film buffs will be intrigued by the exhibits at the **Film Museum Berlin** (open Tues–Sun 10am–6pm, Thur 10am–8pm). This fascinating museum commemorates the city's history as the Hollywood of Germany, and pays tribute to the greatest of all German screen stars, Marlene Dietrich. Also here is the new **Television Museum** covering landmarks in German broadcasting past and present.

Situated to the immediate north of the Sony Center, the 18-storey **Beisheim Center**, housing the Ritz Carlton Hotel, and 17-storey **Delbrück-Haus**, provide a skyline reminiscent of art-deco skyscrapers in New York and Chicago.

Stretching away to the south of the Sony Center, the **Arkaden** shopping centre became a firm favourite with city shoppers as soon as it opened in 1998, and the cafés, casino and theatre in Marlene-Dietrich-Platz are equally popular.

South of Potsdamer Platz

The **Martin-Gropius-Bau**, situated nearby at Stresemann Straße 110, was originally built between 1877 and 1881 by Martin Gropius (great-uncle of the Bauhaus's Walter Gropius), with the help of Heino Schmieden, as an arts and crafts museum. The lavish red and gold building is now a spacious exhibition site housing art and architecture exhibits in and around its skylighted inner courtyard area.

Adjacent to the Martin-Gropius-Bau is the site of Prinz-Albrecht-Straße 8, the former School of Applied Arts and Design, which served as the headquarters of the SS, Gestapo and other Nazi institutions. Excavations in 1987 revealed the cellars where thousands of victims were imprisoned and tortured. The building constructed above the SS guards' under-

Anhalter Bahnhof

Anhalter Bahnhof was once Berlin's most glamorous railway station, linking the city to Europe's other great capitals. Its west-bound platform staged the tragic last act of the Weimar Republic: soon after Hitler became Chancellor, Berlin's most gifted artists and intellectuals – among them Heinrich Mann, Bertolt Brecht, Kurt Weill, Georg Grosz and Albert Einstein – gathered here, their bags packed for the 'last train to freedom'. The station was patched up after the war, but after the border was sealed it stood at the end of a line to nowhere, and became redundant. Today all that remains of Anhalter Bahnhof is the restored entrance portico to the main hall; the land on which the station itself once stood is covered by playing fields and Berlin's tent-like Tempodrom.

ground quarters houses the **Topographie des Terrors**, an exhibition of photographs and documents which movingly illustrates the lives of those who resisted the Nazi terror. Berlin has many reminders of its dark past, but this has particular impact.

Further along at Askanischer Platz is the restored ruin of the entrance portico of **Anhalter Bahnhof**. By an irony of latterday history, the old railway station was the work of Franz Schwechten, the architect who created the Kaiser Wilhelm Memorial Church, that other noble ruin *(see page 32)*.

It's impossible to miss the

Deutsches Technikmuseum, complete with DC3

▶ **Deutsches Technikmuseum Berlin** (U-Bahn Gleisdreieck, S-Bahn Anhalter Bahnhof; open Tues–Fri 9am–5.30pm, Sat–Sun 10am–6pm) on the banks of the Landwehrkanal – poised over its entrance is the front end of one of the original transport planes from the Berlin Airlift, a Douglas DC3. Built over the freight yards of the Anhalter Bahnhof, this is one of the city's most fascinating museums, with a wonderful array of exhibits dealing with all aspects of transport and technology, from railways, aviation, shipping and road transport to textiles, medicine, communications and printing. Visitors to the Spectrum section are encouraged to manipulate various machines and participate in scientific experiments.

Brandenburg Gate

ON AND AROUND UNTER DEN LINDEN

The area east of the Brandenburg Gate, known as Mitte (Middle), is the historic centre of Berlin, and was once the centre of the capital of the German Democratic Republic. The city's most important museums, government buildings churches and theatres were constructed here in the 18th–20th centuries. Many buildings were restored by East Germany after Allied bombing in World War II, and several quarters were almost completely rebuilt in their old style, notably Gendarmenmarkt and Museumsinsel *(see pages 55 and 59)*. Since reunification, restoration has continued apace, facades returned to their former glory and some striking new additions made by internationally acclaimed architects. Today, the area's principal avenue, **Unter den Linden**, has regained its former importance as the main focus of the capital's cultural and political life, while nearby Friedrichstraße is once again Berlin's fashionable shopping artery.

Brandenburg Gate

Once the scene of great military parades and processions, this formidable symbol of the united city appears at last to be realising the vision of Johann Gottfried Schadow, the sculptor who crowned the **Brandenburger Tor** with the Quadriga, a copper statue of Winged Victory in her four-horse chariot. Schadow had wanted the gate to be known as the *Friedenstor* (Gate of Peace), in keeping with the relief of the *Procession of Peace* that he himself had sculpted beneath Victory's simple chariot.

The gate itself, designed by Carl Gotthard Langhans, was built between 1789 and 1791. With two rows of six Doric columns forming the gateway proper, it was inspired by the Propylaeum gatehouse leading to the Parthenon in Athens. Forming part of the city wall, the gate was intended by the pragmatic Prussians not so much as a triumphal arch as an imposing tollgate for collecting duties.

The gate was left isolated in no-man's land when the Wall went up, and subsequently became the scene of quite ecstatic celebrations when the Wall came down, though this may now seem difficult to believe as Berliners walk nonchalantly from east to west through the Brandenburg's mighty central arch.

The north wing of the Gate houses a 'quiet room' where visitors can sit and contemplate in peace; the south wing houses a **BERLIN infostore**.

Jewish memorial

To the south of the Brandenburg Gate, along Friedrich-Ebert-Straße in the direction of Potsdamer Platz, is the Holocaust Mahnmal (memorial), an extensive area of ground planted with 2,700 concrete pillars of differing heights, the concept of the New York architect Peter Eisenman. Deliberately disorientating, the memorial has no designated entrance or exit. There is an information centre underneath.

Pariser Platz

In front of the Brandenburg Gate is the cobbled Pariser Platz, an expansive square surrounded by buildings of varying styles, including the **French Embassy** on the left. On the right looking east, the square is dominated by the smartest hotel in town, the supremely elegant **Hotel Adlon Kempinski**, rebuilt on the site of the original Hotel Adlon, a 1930s Berlin legend. On the square at the side of the Adlon is the controversial

Hotel Adlon Kempinski

glass facade of the new **Akademie der Künste** designed by Günter Behnisch. Next to that, the **DZ Bank** building designed by Californian architect Frank Gehry gives little clue as to what lies inside – a remarkable atrium covered by a vaulted glass roof said to have the form of a fish, beneath which a walk-in sculpture resembling Captain Nemo's *Nautilus* is in fact the outer skin of a conference room. Visitors can go in, but no further than the entrance hall's security turnstiles. Security measures of an entirely different order have also been deployed around the adjacent new **US Embassy**. A passage through the Akademie der Künste leads to the Holocaust Memorial *(see box page 51)*, behind the Embassy.

Unter den Linden to Friedrichstraße

Sweeping eastwards from Pariser Platz, the grand 61m-(200ft-) wide avenue, literally named 'Beneath the Linden Trees', was Berlin's showcase boulevard. Frederick the Great saw it as the centre of his royal capital, and it became the most prestigious address in town. Some of its splendour fell victim to 19th-century building speculation, but the avenue remained fashionable until the bombs of World War II reduced it to rubble. Now the trees have been replanted and most of the important buildings have been restored.

A short distance down on the right is Wilhelmstraße (blocked to traffic by concrete blocks because of security fears). Until World War II this was where the British Embassy was situated, as was the Reichspräsidentenpalais (Palace of the President of the Reich), the Foreign Office, the Reichskanzlei (Chancellery) as well as many other ministries. The **British Embassy** is now back, in a striking new building designed by Michael Wilford and Partners and opened in 2000.

A little further down on the right is the **Russian Federation Embassy**. If you take a right then a left onto Behrenstraße, you'll see the unprepossessing modern facade of the **Komische Oper**, one of Berlin's three opera companies. The ugly exterior is the result of post-war reconstruction; happily, the magnificently over-the-top gilded interior has been retained.

The British Embassy

Friedrichstraße

About half way along, Unter den Linden is crossed by **Friedrichstraße**. Much new building work has been done along this famous street in recent years, both to the north where Friedrichstraße has been restored and to the south where architectural monstrosities built during the days of the GDR have been demolished and replaced by a very elegant development of designer shops, offices and apartments. French élan has come to Berlin in the form of a branch of the famous department store, **Galeries Lafayette**, at Quartier 207. The sophisticated art deco styling of Quartier 206, home to some very exclusive designer boutiques, is the work of Americans Pen, Cobb, Freed and Partners.

Towards the southern end of Friedrichstraße, huge suspended pictures of a Soviet and a US soldier mark the site of **Checkpoint Charlie**, that infamous border crossing between East and West. Six weeks after the building of the Wall, it was here that American and Russian tanks faced each other in what was one of the most tense stand-offs of the Cold War. Today, the barbed wire and barriers are gone, but the memories remain. Right on the spot is an open-air exhibition about the major historic events which took place here. Next to it, the **Haus am Checkpoint Charlie** (U-Bahn Kochstraße; open daily 9am–10pm) celebrates the ingenuity and courage of those who sought to escape to the West, and commemorates those who died while doing so.

Jewish Museum

Jewish Museum

Memories of human tragedy on an even wider scale can be found at the **Jüdisches Museum** (U-Bahn Hallesches Tor; open Mon 10am–10pm, Tues–Sun 10am–8pm), further south on Lindenstraße. With its jagged outline and its disorientating interior of sloping galleries and unexpected angles, Daniel Libeskind's striking zinc-faced building, completed in 1998, symbolises the troubled course of Jewish life in Germany and the devastation of the Holocaust. Its exhibits give a comprehensive and moving account of the long story of German Jewry.

Gendarmenmarkt

From Friedrichstraße follow Jägerstraße or Taubenstraße to reach **Gendarmenmarkt**, the celebrated architectural ensemble south of Unter den Linden. This grand square, bordered by bookshops and cafés set in delightful arcades, has been almost com-

The Deutscher Dom on Gendarmenmarkt

pletely restored after near total destruction during World War II. The imposing **Schiller-Denkmal** (1868), a monument sculpted in Carrara marble, surrounds a statue of the writer Friedrich von Schiller with the muses of philosophy, poetry, drama and history. It stands in front of Schinkel's Ionic-porticoed **Konzerthaus**. Originally called the Schauspielhaus (Playhouse), this is now a concert hall. The edifice stands between two identical churches, the **Französischer Dom** (or French Cathedral) to the north, built for the immigrant Huguenots, and the **Deutscher Dom** (German Cathedral) to the south. Both were built in the early 18th century. The domes were added in 1785.

Step inside the Französischer Dom to visit the **Hugenot-tenmuseum**, or look up the stairwell to the Glockenspiel – a dizzying 48m (159ft) above. The Deutscher Dom now houses a fascinating exhibition, about Germany's recent social and political history. It cleverly combines documents, photographs and radio broadcasts to chronicle the rise of Nazism and the development of democracy. The descriptive panels are all in German, but audio guides and information booklets are available in English and French.

Unter den Linden to Schlossbrücke

East of Charlottenstraße is the patched, dark stone of the **Deutsche Staatsbibliothek** (German State Library), the former Prussian State Library, built between 1903 and 1914 but damaged during World War II. Adjacent is the **Humboldt Universität**. The main building was erected between 1748–66 by Johann Boumann as a palace for Prince Heinrich, the brother of Frederick II. In 1810, on the initiative of the eminent scientists Alexander and Wilhelm von Humboldt, it was converted to a seat of learning. At this point an imposing **statue of Frederick the Great on Horseback** (1851), by Christian Daniel Rauch, stands in the avenue's central strip.

Heinrich's Palace was just part of a grand scheme commissioned by Frederick the Great to recreate the cultural climate that his grandfather had brought to Berlin during the 17th century. Known as the Forum Fridericianum, the major portion of the scheme occupies the other side of

Scholarly greats

Among the renowned academics to work at the Humboldt University were the philosophers Hegel and Schleiermacher, philologists Jacob and Wilhelm Grimm, physicists Max Planck, Albert Einstein and Otto Hahn, physicians Virchow, Koch and Sauerbruch, and many others.

The Neue Wache, built by Karl Friedrich Schinkel

Unter den Linden around the open square called **Bebelplatz** (formerly Opernplatz), which was the scene of book-burning by Nazi students in 1933. On the west side is the curving baroque facade of the **Alte Bibliothek** (Old Library). Facing it to the east is the grand Palladian-style **Staatsoper Unter den Linden** (State Opera) designed in 1742 by von Knobelsdorff, Frederick the Great's favourite architect. To the south of the Staatsoper on the corner of Bebelplatz is **St Hedwigs-Kathedrale**, from 1747, a huge, domed structure built for the Catholics incorporated into Protestant Prussia by Frederick's conquest of Silesia. To the east of the square, the **Operncafé** is housed in the Prinzessinnenpalais, the Prussian princesses' baroque town house. Its open-air terrace is one of the most popular places to meet on Unter den Linden, while inside there is an elegant café and a restaurant to be enjoyed.

Beside the university, the **Neue Wache** (New Guardhouse, open daily 10am–6pm, free) was Karl Friedrich Schinkel's first important building, completed in 1818. After serving as the GDR's 'Memorial to the Victims of Fascism and Militarism', the little neoclassical structure now commemorates all victims of war and tyranny. Inside is Käthe Kollwitz's poignant sculpture *Grieving Mother*.

Next door is the handsome, baroque **Zeughaus**, once arsenal for the Prussian Army, as the sculpted suits of armour testify along the roof. The artist Andreas Schlüter provided the military sculpture, but was able to assert more pacific views with poignant sculpted masks of dying warriors (1696) in the inner courtyard named after him, the **Schlüterhof**. Now splendidly restored and with a glittering annexe by the American architect I.M. Pei, the Zeughaus is the home of the **Deutsches Historisches Museum** (open daily 10am–6pm) with rich collections relating to the country's history.

Architects of Berlin

An outstanding sculptor as well as architect, Andreas Schlüter (1664–1714) was responsible for giving the city much of its baroque appearance. Look for the 21 masks of dying soldiers in the Zeughaus courtyard (Schlüterhof) in Unter den Linden, and the equestrian statue of Friedrich Wilhelm, 'Der Große Kurfürst' (the Great Elector), outside Schloss Charlottenburg.

Georg Wenzeslaus von Knobelsdorff (1699–1753) was Frederick the Great's favourite architect. Among his greatest achievements are St Hedwigs-Kathedrale and the Staatsoper Unter den Linden; the new wing at Schloss Charlottenburg; and Schloss Sanssouci in Potsdam.

Karl Friedrich Schinkel (1781–1841) was Berlin's most gifted and prolific neoclassical architect. His other talents were landscape painting and stage design. Works include the Neue Wache and the Altes Museum, the Schauspielhaus at Gendarmenmarkt, and the neo-Gothic war memorial in Viktoria Park, Kreuzberg.

Linking Unter den Linden to Karl-Liebknecht-Straße is the exquisite **Schlossbrücke** (Palace Bridge), designed by Schinkel in 1820–24 but built after his death in the 1850s, and adorned with fierce warriors and victory goddesses.

Statue on the Schlossbrücke

Museum Island

Beyond the bridge, the imposing neoclassical facade of the Altes Museum at the far end of the Lustgarten (Pleasure Garden), forms a grand entrance to **Museumsinsel** (U-Bahn/ S-Bahn Friedrichstraße, S-Bahn Hackescher Markt), the site of Berlin's most important museums.

The **Altes Museum** (open daily 10am–6pm, Thur 10am–10pm) is a splendid neoclassical building generally regarded as Schinkel's masterpiece. Notice in front the massive polished granite bowl which was originally intended to sit atop the edifice. The museum houses an astonishing collection of Greek and Roman antiquities, and is also the temporary home of the **Egyptian Museum**, until it moves to a permanent home in the Neues Museum in autumn 2009.

This is one of the greatest collections of Egyptian art in Europe, covering 3,000 years of sculpture, papyrus fragments and hieroglyphic tablets. The most famous piece in the collection is undoubtedly the beautiful head of **Queen Nefertiti** (1340BC), consort of Akhenaton. The bust had been buried for over 3,000 years before it was unearthed by German and French archaeologists in 1912. Other highlights of the collection include: the **Berlin Green Head** with its wrin-

NEREUS

Pergamon Altar detail

kled features, mummies and sarcophagi, and blue faience funerary objects in the shape of animals.

Beyond Bodestraße is the **Alte Nationalgalerie** (open Tues–Sun 10am–6pm, Thur 10am–10pm), a temple to 19th-century art. Among the most interesting works are the lively canvases of Carl Blechen. There are also works by Max Liebermann (*The Flax Workers* and portraits of Wilhelm von Bode and Richard Strauss), and by Adolph von Menzel, whose *Eisenwalzwerk* (The Iron Foundry, 1875) is a striking portrayal of industrial labour. Rooms on the upper floor house a fine collection of works by the Romantic painters of the early part of the century; the 24 paintings by Caspar David Friedrich hung here constitute the largest number of works by him to be united under one roof. Among them, look for *Abtei im Eichwald* (Abbey in the Oakwood, 1809) and *Der Mönch am Meer* (The Monk by the Sea, 1810). The Friedrich collection is complemented by 15 of Karl Friedrich Schinkel's paintings: imaginative landscapes and architectural visions.

Further north is the **Pergamonmuseum** (Am Kupfergraben; open daily 10am–6pm, Thur 10am–10pm), home to many impressive works of classical antiquity, the Near East, Islam and the Orient. The museum is named after its most prized possession: the gigantic **Pergamon Altar** (2nd century BC). This masterpiece of Hellenistic art came from what is now Berga-ma, on Turkey's west coast. Dedicated to Zeus and Athena, it has been reconstructed to fill an entire hall of the museum.

The **Babylonian Processional Street** (604–562BC), built by King Nebuchadnezzar II, is equally impressive. Lions sculpted in relief stride along the street's blue-and-ochre tiled walls towards the Ishtar Gate. The gate itself is decorated with bulls and dragons, also in blue-and-ochre tiles.

A third great treasure is the Roman **Market Gate of Mile-tus**, from Greek Asia Minor (AD165). Its name belies the true character of this elaborately pedimented monument, which constitutes both gateway and shopping complex.

The **Islamic Museum** in the Pergamon's south wing exhibits the grand facade of the 8th-century **Palace of Mshatta** (from what is now Jordan). It is embellished with intricately incised or perforated animal and plant motifs. Among the other ex-hibits are some exquisite Indian **Mogul miniatures**.

The final great institution of Museumsinsel, at the very tip of the island, is the **Bodemuseum**. After years of restora-tion, it opened in autumn 2006 to house Early Christian and Byzantine Art, ancient coins, sculpture, and paintings from the Middle Ages to the 18th century.

Berlin Cathedral

On the north side of the Lustgarten stands Kaiser Wilhelm II's **Berliner Dom**. The imposing exterior has been completely re-stored, and its interior beautifully renovated, despite heavy bomb damage in World War II. The cathedral's crypt contains 95 Hohenzollern sarcophagi.

On the other side of the Spree, across the lovely, pedestri-an **Friedrichbrücke**, is the **DDR Museum** (open daily 10am–8pm, Sat until 10pm), which provides an interactive insight into everyday life behind the Wall. Visitors can explore a mock-up DDR apartment and uncover the secrets of the Stasi.

SCHLOSSPLATZ AND BEYOND

On the opposite side of the Lustgarten stands the area once more known as **Schlossplatz**. Under the GDR its name was changed to Marx-Engels-Platz, and it became a focus of Communist May Day military parades and rallies. The war-damaged Stadtschloss (City Palace) of the Hohenzollerns once stood here. However, in 1950 Walter Ulbricht decided to raze it as symbolising German imperialism, despite protests from art historians that it was the city's outstanding baroque building. The palace balcony where Spartacist leader Karl Liebknecht proclaimed his doomed 'Socialist Republic' in 1918 was added to the front of the former **Staatsrat** (Council of State) on the east side of the square, while the monstrous bronze, glass and steel Palast der Republik – once East Germany's parliament – replaced what remained of the royal residence. Today, the decaying Palast is being demolished to make space for the reconstruction of the original palace, which will house the 'Humboldt Forum', an international exhibition of art, culture and science.

Continue along Karl-Liebknecht-Straße as far as the **Marienkirche** (13th century) on Neuer Markt, a

Looking east past the Berliner Dom from Friedrichbrücke

haven of sober Gothic simplicity amid the prevailing bombast. Inside, see Andreas Schlüter's baroque marble pulpit (1703) and a late-Gothic fresco of the *Dance of Death* (1484).

The neo-Renaissance Berliner Rathaus, also known as the **Rotes Rathaus** (Red Town Hall), owes its nickname to its red clinker masonry, not its ideology. Built between 1861 and 1869, it is now the seat of the city's governing mayor, and is

Red Town Hall and TV Tower

decorated with an interesting terracotta frieze chronicling the history of Berlin up to the time of the building's construction.

Alexanderplatz

Beyond the huge **Neptunbrunnen** (Neptune's Fountain) of 1891, an elaborate affair decorated with four figures representing the rivers Rhine, Elbe, Oder and Vistula, you can hardly miss the **Fernsehturm** (Television Tower) rising up above Alexanderplatz. It was built in 1969, and at 365m (1,197ft) dwarfs western Berlin's Funkturm *(see page 72)*, which was the object of the exercise. Not for the fainthearted, an observation deck at 207m (679ft) affords fine views over the city, while the revolving restaurant provides refreshment.

'Alex', as the huge square is known, was the heart of prewar Berlin, and its vibrancy was celebrated in Alfred Döblin's great 1929 novel *Berlin Alexanderplatz*, later filmed by Rainer Werner Fassbinder. Today the square, with its modern fountain and circular World Clock, is undergoing renovation.

Nikolaiviertel

South of the Rotes Rathaus, the Nikolai neighbourhood was restored for Berlin's 750th anniversary celebrations in 1987. The site of Berlin's earliest settlement, the whole district is now a kind of open-air museum. Its focal point is Berlin's oldest church, the twin-steepled Romanesque and Gothic **Nikolaikirche**, begun in 1230. Among the buildings resurrected here is the **Gaststätte zum Nußbaum**, the favourite tavern of cartoonist Heinrich Zille. Some of his works can be seen in the **Heinrich Zille Museum Berlin** close by (Propststraße 11). The **Knoblauchhaus**, at Poststraße 23, is an elegant house rebuilt in neoclassical style in 1835 and containing some fine Biedermeier furniture. More stately is the reconstructed Ephraimpalais (Poststraße 16), a rococo mansion built for Friedrich II's financier Veitel Heine Ephraim in 1765. Today the **Museum Ephraim-Palais** presents exhibitions of the history of Berlin's arts and culture on three floors.

Märkisches Museum

On the other side of the Spree, across the Jannowitzbrücke, stands the red-brick **Märkisches Museum** (U-Bahn Märkisches Museum; open Tues–Sun 10am–6pm). With a wealth of exhibits, the museum tells the story of Berlin from the Middle Ages to the present. Odd bits of Berliniana include early sewing machines, bicycles, telephones, and an 1881 phone book with just 41 names. The building itself is worthy of attention – its Gothic chapel, guildhall and arms hall have all been restored to their original state.

The nearby **Fischerinsel** is one of the oldest parts of Berlin/Cölln, but you wouldn't guess it now. The medieval houses that survived World War II were demolished in the 1960s, and the island is now dominated by residential tower blocks. Along the **Märkisches Ufer**, however, is the Historical Harbour, a collection of old barges that once plied the Spree.

Oranienburger Straße

On the north side of the River Spree, **Oranienburger Straße** is the heart of the old Jewish quarter. In the 1920s, a diverse community of Jewish professionals and bohemian artists and writers lived, worked and thrived here. After the devastation of the war and the grim sterility of its aftermath, the area has now regained much of its former vibrancy, with cultural centres and Jewish restaurants rubbing shoulders with off-beat cafés and alternative art venues beneath the magnificent black-and-gold-leafed dome of the **Neue Synagoge**. The

The Neue Synagoge

biggest synagogue in Germany, designed by Eduard Knoblauch and completed in 1866, it was saved during the anti-Semitic attacks of *Kristallnacht* on 9 November 1938 *(see page 22)* but later destroyed by Allied bombing. It has now been beautifully restored, and is used for services once more. In addition, exhibits from the adjacent centre of Jewish studies, Centrum Judaicum, are displayed here.

Nearby **Hackesche Höfe** is a fascinating complex of early 20th-century courtyards. Beautifully restored, this is now a lively spot, with bars, art galleries, shops and offices, and even a theatre. The Adjacent **Anne Frank Zentrum** features an exhibition devoted to the life of Anne Frank (S-Bahn Hackescher Markt; open Tues–Sun noon–8pm).

Berlin Beer Festival

On the first weekend in August a 1,600m (1-mile) stretch of Karl-Marx-Allee is transformed into the world's longest beer garden with the arrival of the Berlin Beer Festival. Brewers from across Germany, as well as from Poland, the Czech Republic, Belgium and the UK, set up their stalls on the broad verges, and stages with live music and shows provide entertainment.

Karl-Marx-Allee

Known until 1961 as Stalin-Allee, **Karl-Marx-Allee** runs southeast from Alexanderplatz. It is worth coming here to look at the facades of the **Stalinesque-style apartment blocks** that line the avenue on both sides, and which, as far as Frankfurter Tor, have been superbly restored. Whether or not you're a fan of the style, you have to be impressed by the sheer scale of the enterprise.

South of Karl-Marx-Allee along Mühlenstraße, between Ostbahnhof and Oberbaumbrücke, a section of the Berlin Wall has been preserved as the **East Side Gallery**. A variety of international artists painted murals here in 1990, after the collapse of the Wall, and some of them have since been restored. You can still see some of the iconic images of that era, including *Brotherly Kiss* by Dimitri Vrubel, depicting Leonid Brezhnev and Erich Honecker in fond embrace.

Prenzlauer Berg

To the north of Alexanderplatz, Schönhauser Allee leads to the centre of **Prenzlauer Berg**, a 19th-century working-class quarter – now a lively, bohemian area with colourful nightlife, plenty of cafés and restaurants, and entertainment complexes such as the **Kulturbrauerei**, a converted brewery. The artist Käthe Kollwitz *(see page 31)* lived in Prenzlauer Berg; a colourful market is held around the central Kollwitzplatz every Thursday and Saturday.

BEYOND THE CENTRE

Schloss Charlottenburg

An exemplary piece of Prussian baroque and rococo architecture and decoration, **Schloss Charlottenburg** is the city's only surviving major Hohenzollern residence. Badly damaged in a World War II air raid, it became the target of extensive post-war reconstruction, and is now the focal point of a number of the city's most fascinating museums. To do the palace, grounds and surrounding museums full justice, you will need to spend at least a day here.

Schloss Charlottenburg was conceived as a summer retreat for the future Queen Sophie Charlotte in the 1690s, when the site beside the River Spree, west of the Tiergarten, lay well outside the city limits. It was a small palace – scarcely one-fifth of the huge structure you see today – and only with the

Schloss Charlottenburg

Fine furnishings

To try and recapture the interior's rather gracious rococo atmosphere, furniture and decorations from other Prussian palaces built in the 18th century have been used to replace what was destroyed at Charlottenburg during World War II.

addition of a majestic domed tower (with the goddess Fortune as its weathervane), the Orangerie to the west and a new east wing, did it become big enough for Frederick the Great. If he ever had to leave his beloved Potsdam, this was where he came.

In the palace courtyard you will find an **equestrian statue** of the Great Elector Friedrich Wilhelm, designed by Schlüter in 1697. One of many art works lost in World War II, it was finally recovered from Tegel Lake in 1949, where it had sunk with the barge that was taking it to safety.

In the **Gobelinzimmer**, notice the fine 18th-century tapestries by Charles Vigne. The rays of light on the ceiling of the **Audienzzimmer** (Reception Room) and bright yellow damask walls in the **Schlafzimmer** (bedroom) imitate the motif of the Sun King, Louis XIV, the Prussian rulers' hero. Chinoiserie is the dominating feature of the opulent **Porzellankabinett**, filled with hundreds of pieces of Chinese and Japanese porcelain. The relatively sober **Japanische Kammer** contains some prized lacquered cabinets and tables, as well as tapestries which actually depict landscapes in China. The **Eichengalerie** (Oak Gallery) is filled with portraits of the Hohenzollern family. Chamber music recitals can be heard in the **Eosander-Kapelle** (chapel), which has extravagant rococo decor that makes it more like a theatre than a place of worship.

Designed for Frederick the Great by Georg von Knobelsdorff, the **Neuer Flügel** (new wing, also the east wing) subtly combines dignified late-baroque facades with exuberant rococo interiors. The ceremonial staircase which leads to

Frederick the Great's state apartments has an abstract modern ceiling fresco by Hann Trier in place of the original decor which was destroyed by fire. Trier also painted the ceiling of the **Weiße Saal** (throne room and banquet hall).

The finest achievement of Knobelsdorff at Schloss Charlottenburg is the 42m- (138-ft-) long **Goldene Galerie**. This rococo ballroom, with its marble walls and gilded stucco, leads to two rooms containing a fine group of **Watteau paintings**. Frederick the Great was somewhat amused by the French artist's insolent *Enseigne du Gersaint*, a shop sign for art dealer Gersaint, in which a portrait of Louis XIV is being unceremoniously packed away. Among various other fine works by Watteau, you will find *L'amour paisible* (Quiet Love) and *Les Bergers* (The Shepherds).

Statue in the grounds

The new wing's first floor was recently converted into a modern exhibition hall, with high-tech facilities.

Take a break for coffee or lunch at the **Kleine Orangerie**, then head off and explore the **Schlosspark**. Among the many buildings in the grounds, nearest to the palace is the Italian-style **Schinkel-Pavillon** (1825), which is closed for restoration until 2010. North of the carp pond, the elegant **Belvedere**, once a teahouse, now houses a collection of exquisite 18th- and 19th-century porcelain. Also worth visiting in the park is Queen Louise's mausoleum with her marble sarcophagus inside. The 200th anniversary of her death will be commemorated in 2010.

The west wing of the palace, which was constructed as a theatre, now houses the **Museum für Vor- und Frühgeschichte** (Museum of Prehistory and Early History, open Tues–Fri 9am–5pm, Sat–Sun 10am–5pm) with an extensive collection of artefacts from the Stone Age to the Bronze Age. Highlights of the display include a renowned collection of Trojan antiquities, the famed Berlin gold hat and copies of gold objects held in Russia since 1945, among them the pre-Christian treasure discovered in Eberswalde.

Opposite the palace are the two so-called 'Stüler buildings'. The western one is the home of the **Museum Berggruen** (open Tues–Sun 10am–6pm), an outstanding collection of late 19th- and early 20th-century art assembled by the Berlin-born art-lover Heinz Berggruen (1914–2007). There are works by many of the great masters of Modernism, while the heart of the collection is formed by dozens of pieces by Picasso. The eastern building is home to the **Sammlung Scharf-Gerstenberg** (open Tues–Sun 10am–6pm), a collection of Surrealist art. The collection includes paintings, sculptures and drawings by artists such as Goya, Klinger, Redon, Dalí, Magritte, Ernst and Klee. The art is accompanied by a film programme which includes the classic Surrealist films of Salvador Dalí and Luis Buñuel, as well as films by contemporary artists who draw upon Surrealism.

The private **Bröhan Museum** (open Tues–Sun 10am–6pm), dedicated to art nouveau and art deco, is housed in a former infantry barracks opposite the eastern Stüler building. Its peaceful interior makes a fine setting for the array of elegant objects amassed by businessman Karl Bröhan from the 1960s onwards. Highlights include superb ceramics, glassware, silverware and furniture.

Olympic Stadium

Built for the Games of 1936, Hitler's Olympiastadion was spared bombardment to serve as headquarters for the British Army. The structure's bombastic gigantism is an eloquent testimony to the Führer's taste in architecture. Viewed from the main Olympic Gate, it appears surprisingly 'low slung' until you see that the field itself has been sunk 12m (40ft) below ground level. The 76,000-capacity stadium still stages sporting events, and is open daily to the public at other times (10am–7pm in summer, 10am–4pm in winter). In preparation for the football World Cup in 2006 the stadium was elaborately modernised and equipped with a new roof covering all the seating.

West of the stadium, the **Glockenturm** (bell tower) gives a magnificent view over the Olympic site. Beyond the tower, a pathway leads to the **Waldbühne**, an open-air amphitheatre which is a summer venue for concerts and films.

The Olympic Stadium with its new roof

On Messedamm, southeast of the stadium, stands another colossus, the famous **ICC** *(International Congress Centre)*. One of the biggest convention centres in the world, the complex is also used for staging cultural events. Next to it on the equally huge **Messe und Ausstellungsgelände** (Trade Fair and Exhibition Area), the **Funkturm** (Radio Tower) is positively tiny – 150m (492ft) to the tip of its antenna, less than half the height of the Television Tower at Alexanderplatz *(see page 63)*. For breathtaking views, take the lift to the restaurant, 55m (180ft) up, or to the observation platform all the way at the top.

Gedenkstätte Plötzensee

Northeast of Charlottenburg, the **Gedenkstätte Plötzensee** in Hüttigpfad is a stark and moving memorial to the victims of Nazi persecution (take bus TXL from Hauptbahnhof to Plötzensee). On the opposite side of the road a lane leads to the site of the prison where thousands of people were tortured and executed between 1933 and 1945, including many of the officers involved in the Stauffenberg plot to kill Hitler.

The dark sheds where executions were carried out have been preserved, and outside a stone urn, filled with soil from concentration camps, stands in a corner of the yard. In one of the sheds you will find a small and poignant exhibition of historical documents which includes death warrants and pictures of leading members of the German resistance. There is an information office where you can obtain free booklets in English, French and Russian.

Execution shed at Plötzensee

Dahlem

The history of leafy Dahlem probably goes back for more than 750 years, and something of its rustic character remains, to which the thatched and half-timbered U-Bahn station makes its contribution. Opposite the station is one of Berlin's oldest buildings, a manor house of 1560 which is part of the **Domäne Dahlem**, a visitor-friendly rural estate with old buildings, a museum, farm animals, well-tended fields, traditional crafts and carriage rides. Dahlem is also an academic and museum district; it was chosen as the site of the Free University set

Museen Dahlem

up during the 1948 Airlift as an alternative to the Humboldt University in the Soviet sector of the city, and it is home to some of Berlin's finest museums.

The main complex is known as the **Museen Dahlem** (Lansstraße 8; U-Bahn Dahlem-Dorf; open Tues–Fri 10am–6pm, Sat–Sun 11am–6pm). It consists of four museums housing a huge range of art and crafts from around the world. The **Museum für Asiatische Kunst** (Museum of Asian Art) displays treasures from China, Japan and Korea, including delicate paper hangings, wooden screens, paintings, carpets, ceramics and lacquerware; and there is a room devoted to Buddhist art from all three countries. The **Museum für Indische Kunst** (Museum of Indian Art) is devoted to art and crafts from Pak-

Botanical garden

Berlin's superlative Botanischer Garten (Königin-
Luise-Straße 6–8; S-Bahn
Botanischer Garten; open
9am–dusk) is also in
Dahlem. Its tropical houses
contain some 18,000
species of exotic plants and
there is also a smell and
touch garden for the blind.
A small museum at the
north entrance covers the
history and use of plants.

istan, Afghanistan, Sri Lanka, Nepal, Tibet, Southeast Asia and Central Asia, and includes a fine selection of Buddhist sculpture. The **Ethnologisches Museum** (Ethnological Museum) focuses on the cultures of ancient America, the South Seas, and South and East Asia, with a special section on Native North Americans and a spectacular presentation on art from Africa. At the rear, the **Museum Europäischer Kulturen** (Arnimallee 25; open Tues–Fri 10am–6pm, Sat–Sun 11am– 6pm) deals with the folk culture of European peoples, with displays of tools, clothes, toys and much else.

The **Brücke-Museum** (Bus 115 to Pücklerstraße from U-Bahn Oskar-Helene-Heim, then 5 mins on foot; open Tues–Sun 11am–5pm) houses a number of fine works by early 20th-century German artists. It was founded in 1967 thanks to a legacy of Karl Schmidt-Rottluff, a member of the Expressionist group *Die Brücke* which worked in Dresden from 1905 to 1913. A large number of the group's works were labelled as 'degenerate' and thus destroyed by the Nazis. Schmidt-Rottluff's own bold paintings hang beside the works of fellow Expressionists Emil Nolde, Erich Heckel, Ernst Ludwig Kirchner and Max Pechstein.

Grunewald and Wannsee

On the western edge of Berlin, the dense pine forest which was largely stripped for fuel in 1945 has been replanted, adding to the 18 million pines around six million chestnut, linden, beech, birch and oak trees. The lush wooded areas form a reserve for deer, wild boar, marten, foxes and rabbits, but there are also plenty of green meadows for picnics, and the forest paths are extremely popular with both cyclists and joggers.

The easiest and most direct way to get to the Grunewald is to take the S-Bahn from Bahnhof Zoo to Grunewald S-Bahn station. Alternatively, you could combine your trip with a visit to the museums at Dahlem – the Brücke Museum is only a 20-minute walk from the eastern edge of the forest. Drivers take the Avus and turn off on the Hüttenweg to **Grunewaldsee**, a lake offering swimming and sandy beaches. On the east shore, in an attractive lakeside setting of beech trees, you will find the **Jagdschloss Grunewald**, a hunting lodge built in 1542 for Prince Elector Joachim II. Situated in a cobbled courtyard, the lodge has been restored to its original Renaissance appearance.

Jagdschloss Grunewald

The lodge will reopen after extensive renovation in June 2009, showing an exhibition about Berlin portrait painting throughout the centuries. The permanent collection of early German hunting portraits and landscapes, which includes a series of panels depicting the Passion Cycle by Lucas Cranach, as well as works by Jordaens, Rubens and Bruyn, will not be on display until 2011.

Despite the restoration work, the small hunting museum on the opposite side of the courtyard is still displaying its collection dedicated to 'the royal hunt'. Numerous finds from excavations of the former moat, dating back to the 16th century, will be on display for the first time. A short walk down the path outside the lodge brings you to the rather grand **Forsthaus Paulsborn**, where you can dine in splendour overlooking the lake.

On the Grunewald's west side, along Havelchaussee, the **Grunewaldturm** (Grunewald Tower) is a neo-Gothic tower built in 1897 to commemorate the 100th anniversary of the birth of Wilhelm I. You can climb the 205 steps to reach the 55m- (180ft-) high observation platform for views as far as Potsdam. Ferry stations in the area offer boat rides on the River Havel and forest lakes, and the east bank of the Havel is lined with sandy beaches as far as the Wannsee lakes.

The waterfront near **Wannsee** S-Bahn station is a crowded spot where city-dwellers come and let their hair down on warm spring and summer days. The water bustles with pleas-

Teufelsberg – Devil's Mountain

At the beginning of the Grunewald, in the middle of the flat, northern European plain that stretches from Warsaw to the Netherlands, is a mountain. Aptly named Teufelsberg (Devil's Mountain), it is not tall – only 115m (380ft) – but a mountain nevertheless, painstakingly created from a pile of rubble from World War II bombardments.

In summer, the hill is nicely grassed over for toddler mountain climbers to scramble on. In winter, snow creates an excellent toboggan run, a good nursery slope for skiers, and even two bone-rattling ski jumps. The flatness of the north European plain east of the mountain is demonstrated by the off-limits summit where military radar equipment used to operate as far as Asia.

ure boats and ferries, and you can cruise all the way to Potsdam from here. **Strandbad Wannsee** is Berlin's biggest beach, and the longest inland one in Europe.

To the west of the Großer Wannsee, Königstraße crosses Berliner Forst, an extension of the Grunewald to **Glienicke Park**. Its whimsical landscaping of little hills, bridges and ponds was the work of Peter Josef Lenné in the early 19th century. **Schloss Glienicke** (1828) is a rather austere neoclassical edifice, but the nearby cloister, villa and garden houses add a romantic touch.

Ferry across the Wannsee

A ferry links **Pfaueninsel** (Peacock Island), a delightfully tranquil nature reserve in the Havel, towards the northern edge of Berliner Forst. The island menagerie was used to stock the Berlin Zoo, but the bird sanctuary still has much to offer the nature-lover including, of course, peacocks.

At the southern tip, half hidden in the trees, is Schinkel's Swiss Cottage, but the island's principal curiosity is the fake ruin **Schloss Pfaueninsel**, built in 1797 as a hideaway for Friedrich Wilhelm II and his lover, the Countess Wilhelmine von Lichtenau. The white wooden facade imitates granite blocks, and the delightful turrets are joined together at the top by a pretty bridge.

Königsstraße extends as far as an illustrious relic of the Cold War, **Glienicker Bridge**, once a restricted border crossing between West Berlin and East Germany where the KGB and CIA exchanged spies.

The garden front of Schloss Sanssouci

POTSDAM

A visit to the elegant old baroque town of Potsdam is recommended. Potsdam, which is much older than Berlin (it was first mentioned as Poztupimi in AD993), is situated 30km (19 miles) southwest of the city. You can get there from central Berlin in a number of ways, of which the quickest is by Regional Express train from Bahnhof Zoo to Potsdam Hauptbahnhof. S-Bahn Line 7 also runs to Potsdam Hauptbahnhof. You could get off the S-Bahn at Wannsee and continue by boat, or take Bus 316 to Glienicker Brücke and continue by Tram 93 to Potsdam town centre. From Potsdam Hauptbahnhof, visitors heading straight for Sanssouci should take the 695 bus.

Park Sanssouci

Potsdam's main attractions are the summer palaces and gardens at Sanssouci, built in the 18th and 19th centuries. The vast grounds are filled with charming palaces, pavilions, fountains and temples. **Schloss Sanssouci** (open Tues–Sun 9am–5pm, 4pm in winter; reservation necessary) was commissioned by Frederick the Great and designed by von Knobelsdorff in 1744 from the king's own sketches. Despite only being single-storey, the 97m- (300ft-) garden front is very impressive, with its floor-to-ceiling windows and a total of 35 huge caryatids supporting the roof and dome architrave. Highlights of the magnificent rococo interior include Frederick's splendid **Konzertsaal** (Concert Chamber) where walls and ceiling are overlaid with a delicate gilt filigree; at the centre of the palace, beneath the dome, the **Marmorsaal** (Marble Hall) contains exquisite columns made from Carrara marble and stucco figures perched high up on the cornice. Among the guest rooms, the yellow **Voltaire room** boasts bizarre rococo decorations including wooden parrots hanging from perches.

Nearby, the **Bildergalerie** (Picture Gallery; open Tues–Sun 10am–5pm, closed in winter) was designed to house Frederick the Great's collection of paintings by masters such as Caravaggio and Rubens. A path through the woods southwest of the palace leads to the **Chinesisches Haus** (open Tues–Sun 10am–5pm, closed in winter). On top sits a gilded mandarin under a sunshade; more statues surround the base. Inside, you'll find a collection of Chinese porcelain.

A gilded mandarin sits atop the Chinese House

At the far western end of the Hauptallee stands the **Neues Palais** (New Palace, open Sat–Thur 9am–5pm), a vast structure built in the 1760s from red brick and white sandstone, which is covered in rococo statuary. It contains a rich collection of furniture, paintings by Italian, Dutch and French baroque and rococo masters, as well as some fine 18th-century ceiling frescoes.

Other highlights of the park include the **Römische Bäder** (Roman Baths) by Schinkel, and **Schloss Charlottenhof**. To the north is the vast Italian Renaissance-style **Orangerie**.

Reflections in Park Sanssouci

Schloss Cecilienhof

Beside a lake, north of the town centre, is **Neuer Garten**, a pleasant English-style park. It provides the perfect setting for **Schloss Cecilienhof** (1916), the ivy-covered, half-timbered pastiche of an English country manor built for Crown Prince Wilhelm and his wife. Winston Churchill, Joseph Stalin and Harry Truman met here in July 1945 to draw up the Potsdam Agreement that fixed the division of Germany for the next 45 years. Today it's a luxury hotel and museum. Another jewel in the Neuer Garten is the neoclassical **Marmorpalast** (Marble Palace).

Town Centre Attractions

Arriving in Potsdam by boat or train, the first major building you'll see, dominating the Alter Markt, is the neoclassical **Nikolaikirche**. Designed by Karl-Friedrich Schinkel, its dome bears a striking resemblance to that of St Paul's Cathedral in London. Opposite, on the other side of the Havel, stands the baroque Town Hall, completed in 1753. The old town, which is full of fine baroque townhouses, has three historic gates, the Brandenburger Tor (1770), the Jägertor (1773) and the Nauenertor (1755). Beyond the latter lies the attractive **Holländische Viertel** (Dutch quarter), built between 1734 and 1741 by Jan Boumann, for Dutch settlers.

Einstein Tower

To the south of the town centre, Albert-Einsteinstraße climbs Telegrafenberg to the bizarre **Einsteinturm** (open for guided tours Oct–Mar), built in 1921 as an astrophysics observatory. Albert Einstein was present here at a memorable technical demonstration of his Theory of Relativity. The observatory is still in use today, and for want of a fitting statue to the great man, staff have placed in the entrance hall, as a splendidly atrocious visual pun, a simple small stone – Ein Stein.

Babelsberg

The suburb of **Babelsberg**, to the east of Potsdam, was home to the film industry which rivalled Hollywood in the 1920s. Classics such as Fritz Lang's *Metropolis* were made here. Now run as a studio and theme park, **Filmpark Babelsberg** (open Apr–Oct daily 10am–6pm) organises guided tours. You will also find vintage cars and stunt shows here.

Other excursions

Other worthwhile excursion destinations within greater Berlin itself include Spandau, on the northwestern edge of the city, with its restored Altstadt (old town) and 16th-century citadel in the river Havel. In the far southeast is Köpenick, which grew up around a 9th-century Slav settlement in the Spree. The local Schloss houses a Museum of Arts and Crafts; nearby Großer Müggelsee is Berlin's largest lake.

WHAT TO DO

In this liveliest of German cities, there is no lack of activities once your sightseeing is done; Berlin has never relinquished its role as the country's capital of the arts or shopping.

ENTERTAINMENT

Berliners are the most assiduous concert- and theatre-goers in Europe, and you have to plan ahead if you want good tickets for the main events. Ask at a travel agency or tourist office about upcoming programmes, and book in advance where possible. In addition to the monthly publication *Berlin Programm*, there are two listings magazines, *Tip* and *Zitty*, published every two weeks, which give full details and reviews. *Berlin To Go* is a weekly listings magazine with detailed information on cultural events. *The Exberliner* is Berlin's English-language paper, published monthly (<www.exberliner.com>). Tickets and information are available on the Berlin Tourism Organisation's website: <www.berlin-tourist-information.de>.

Music

Symphonic music in Berlin centres on the Berliner Philharmoniker, one of the world's greatest orchestras, with Sir Simon Rattle as chief conductor. It is housed in the Philharmonie *(see page 44)*. Other renowned orchestras also perform there, such as the Berliner Staatskapelle under Daniel Barenboim, and the Deutsches Symphonie-Orchester Berlin. Schinkel's beautifully restored Schauspielhaus on Gendarmenmarkt (known as the Konzerthaus Berlin, *see page 55*) is another important venue for classical music performances.

The striking Philharmonie, home of the Berlin Philharmonic

Chamber music and *Lieder* (song) recitals take place in the Kammermusiksaal (at the rear of the Philharmonie) and the Universität der Künste, Hardenbergstraße 33.

Berlin's **opera** lovers are well served by the Deutsche Oper in Bismarckstraße, the Staatsoper Unter den Linden and the Komische Oper in Behrenstraße.

Major **rock** concerts are usually performed in big halls such as the Max-Schmeling-Halle, the Velodrom, the open-air Waldbühne and the Olympic Stadium. **Jazz** is particularly popular in Berlin. Venues include Quasimodo (Kantstraße 12a) and A-Trane Jazzclub (Bleibtreustraße 1). Jazzfest Berlin is an annual jazz festival held in the city each November.

Theatre

When it comes to theatre, Berlin is one of the most exciting and innovative cities in Europe. There are over 150 theatres in the city, and even without a great command of the German language any enthusiastic theatregoer can enjoy some stirring performances. Major theatres often maintain several productions in repertory, so that in any one week you will be able to see the same troupe perform contemporary or classical drama.

The city's most controversial theatre performances are staged at the Volksbühne (Rosa-Luxemburg-Platz), while the Schaubühne (Ku'damm and Lehninerplatz) achieved international renown for its uncompromising performances of classical avant-garde and experimental theatre. The plays of Berlin's best-known playwright, Bertolt Brecht, are still performed at the theatre he founded, the world-renowned Berliner Ensemble (Bertolt-Brecht-Platz 1), although it does expand to other, mostly modern, classics. **Contemporary plays** are staged at the Maxim-Gorki-Theater (Am Festungsgraben 2), and the **classics** at the Deutsches Theater (Schumannstraße 13a), the former home of theatre producer Max Reinhardt. The English Theatre Berlin (Kreuzberg, Fidicinstraße 40)

Staatsoper Unter den Linden

offers a wide variety of quality English-language theatre, including classics, new writing, physical theatre and comedy.

For **popular theatre**, such as musicals, operettas and comedies, try the very professional Theater am Kurfürstendamm (Kurfürstendamm 209), the adjacent Komödie (Kurfürstendamm 206), the popular Theater des Westens (Kantstraße 12), the Musical Theater (Marlene-Dietrich-Platz 1), as well as the Admiralspalast (Friedrichstraße 101).

Berlin's largest audience magnet is the **Friedrichstadtpalast**, the only revue theatre in Germany and the largest in Europe. Each production is produced exclusively for the location and performed by the house troupe and orchestra.

Other Entertainment

Another long-standing tradition, at its heyday in the 1920s, satirical cabaret has always, by its very nature, had to struggle for existence. Survivors among countless fly-by-nights in-

Night lights at the Sony Center

clude *Die Stachelschweine* (Europa-Center) and *Die Distel* (Friedrichstraße 101). However, unless your German is excellent, this kind of cabaret will be almost impossible to follow. Bar jeder Vernunft (Schaperstraße 24) and Tipi (close to the Chancellery) offer more music-orientated programmes.

A feature of Berlin are **transvestite shows**, which can be saucy, often witty, occasionally outrageous, but rarely offensive. Berlin has an Erotic Theatre situated at Potsdamer Platz. The shows at the 'Belle et Fou' Theatre combine dance, music, comedy and artistic acts with subtle eroticism, and promise a unique 'theatre of the senses'.

Nightclubs range from the conventional to the downright weird. Trendy places include Neunzig Grad in Schöneberg with its high-energy music, the Tresor in an old power plant on Köpenicker Straße, and the Sage Club, also on Köpenicker Straße (Mitte), with its three dance floors, special pool area and fire-breathing dragon.

As befits a city which every February hosts a major international film festival, Berlin is endowed with a huge number of **cinemas**, showing everything from Hollywood blockbusters to avant-garde works of art. Most foreign-language films are dubbed into German, though some cinemas will show films in the original language (*Originalfassung* – OF).

SHOPPING

Where to Shop

Each of Berlin's many districts has its own shopping area, but the city's retail heart remains in the west, on and around the Kurfürstendamm. The Ku'damm itself is lined with trendy boutiques and large department stores such as **Wertheim**. The most famous international designer labels and some exquisite jewellers have luxurious stores on the Ku'damm, particularly between Bleibtreustraße and Olivaer Platz. The cherished institution of **KaDeWe** on Wittenbergplatz, the **Europa-Center** multi-storey mall and the redeveloped **Kranzler Eck** with its striking glass skyscraper are close at hand, while elegant shopping streets lead off to the north and south, with a particular focus around Savignyplatz.

In the east, shoppers crowd Friedrichstraße in search of designer labels. The complex of stylish malls known as the Friedrichstraße Passagen are always busy, and the glittering premises of **Galeries Lafayette** offer an injection of French style. The streets and courtyards north of **Hackescher Markt** have been colonised by a fascinating mixture of fashion boutiques, galleries, antique dealers and bookshops. At the junction of east and west, Potsdamer Platz boasts **Arkaden**, a large indoor shopping centre with 100-plus shops and supermarkets.

Doll in KaDeWe

Most of the city's shops are open from 9 or 10am until 8pm Monday to Saturday. However, many shops, especially in quiet neighbourhoods, may close earlier. Shops are allowed to open from 1–8pm on Sundays in Advent, as well as on six further Sundays during the year.

What to Buy
Antiques

Any moderately priced furniture or porcelain that claims to be baroque or rococo is probably a copy. Your best bet is to concentrate on products of the 19th and early 20th centuries. Try looking along some of the side streets off the Ku'damm like Fasanenstraße.

Books

Big general bookshops like Hugendubel (Friedrichstraße 83 and Tauentzienstraße 13) and Dussmann (Friedrichstraße 90) are lavishly stocked and have some English-language books. Marga Schoeller Bücherstube (Knesebeckstraße 33) has a small, interesting English section. Specialist English-language bookshops include Books in Berlin (Goethestraße 69) and Village Voice (Ackerstraße 1a), which also has a café. The bookstore Berlin Story (Unter den Linden 26; open Mon–Sat 10am–10pm, Sun 10am–8pm) is devoted exclusively to 'Berlin' and offers about 300 English-language titles dealing with everything from Prussian kings and Third Reich history to modern architecture. The capital is also home to second-hand

Gift Hunting in Museums

Museum shops are a good place to find art posters, lithographs and high-quality reproductions. In museums of classical antiquity such as the Ägyptisches Museum and the Pergamon, you can get excellent copies of Greek vases or ancient sculpture in bronze, plaster or resin. Museum shops also offer a certain guarantee of quality for genuine artisan products such as textiles, pottery, pewter and woodcarving.

and antiquarian bookshops, especially on Schlüterstraße and Knesebeckstraße.

Bric-a-brac

Collectors of faded old photos, period clothes and other souvenirs from the past will love rummaging around in Berlin's many flea markets. Among the best is the Berliner Antik- und Flohmarkt located in the S-Bahn arches beneath Friedrichstraße station (closed Tues). A huge selection of second-hand records, *objets d'art* and clothes can be found at the weekend flea market on the Straße des 17. Juni in Charlottenburg. Another popular weekend

Flea market on Kupfergraben

flea market, specialising in art objects, books and records, is the one held on the Kupfergraben opposite the Museumsinsel. Head to the Turkish Market *(Türkischer Wochenmarkt)* on the Landwehr canal's Maybachufer in Kreuzberg for all manner of wares, as well as to try exotic food, and buy spices and utensils (open Tues and Fri afternoons).

Gourmet Delicacies

If you want to take back an edible souvenir, check your country's regulations governing the import of certain types of food. Among the pastries and cakes which travel best are *Lebkuchen* (gingerbread), *Spekulatius* (spiced Christmas cookies) and marzipan. KaDeWe's *Feinschmeckeretage* (gourmet floor) of-

fers 500 different breads and 1,500 different types of cheese, plus rare eastern delicacies, exotic teas, handmade chocolates and Beluga caviar. Berlin has no local wine, but plenty of wine shops to satisfy all connoisseurs of the best Rhine, Mosel and Baden Württemberg vintages.

Music, Videos and Cameras

The land of Bach and Beethoven offers a range of CDs, records and tapes second only to that of the US. One of the best places to go for classical recordings is Musikhaus Riedl at Uhlandstraße 38.

Galeries Lafayette facade

Porcelain and Linen

Look for modern Rosenthal and the local Königliche Porzellan Manufaktur (KPM), which was launched by Frederick the Great in the 18th century. The KPM shop on the factory premises (at Straße des 17 Juni 100) also sells reduced-price seconds. Other celebrated manufacturers represented in Berlin, and particularly in the antiques shops, are Meissen (at the Hilton Hotel), Nymphenburg of Munich and Frankenthal.

Bed- and table-linens in Germany are of the finest quality. The duck- or goose-down *Federbett* (duvet) is a lifetime investment. Apart from the warm-as-toast winter model, look for the lightweight one designed for summer use, which is equally comfy.

SPORTS

The lakes and rivers in and around Berlin provide endless opportunities for **watersports** of all kinds. It's easy to rent equipment for waterskiing, canoeing, rowing, sailing and windsurfing. Swimmers have around 20 beaches at their disposal, most of them pleasantly sandy. Continuing the old Prussian devotion to physical culture, a few of the beaches are reserved for nude bathing – or FKK, as you may see it signposted. The most popular of these beaches are the Bullenwinkel on the Grunewaldsee, Strandbad Halensee and the Teufelssee. If you would rather wear a swimming costume, try the lovely beaches of the Wannsee, Glienicker See, the Havel, or the less crowded Großer Müggelsee, far in the east of Berlin, and Templiner See, out at Potsdam.

Alternatively, swimmers can head for the Schwimm- und Sprunghalle in Europasportpark (Paul-Heyse-Straße 26, Prenzlauer Berg) or the beautiful, ornate Stadtbad Neukölln. The 'Kinderbad Monbijou' in the park opposite the Bode-Museum is a safe pool for small children. Many luxury hotels have pools and spa facilities for recreation.

Berlin's sports facilities are second to none, thanks in large part to the huge programme of building that took place as part of the city's unsuccessful bid for the 2000 Olympics. There are over 1,500 sports venues in the city, most impressive of which are the Max-Schmeling-Halle and the Velodrom (both in the Prenzlauer Berg district).

Sailing on the Wannsee

Golf enthusiasts can get a round in at the Golf und Landclub Berlin-Wannsee Club (Golfweg 22), as well as at the Golf Club Gatow in Spandau.

Tennis is a favourite national sport, and **squash** and **badminton** are also popular. All three are well served, so to speak, at courts citywide, notably Stromstraße and Brandenburgische Straße.

One surprise sport you may not have expected to practise in Berlin is **hang-gliding**, but it is, in fact, possible to throw yourself off the Teufelsberg, where you can also do a little **skiing** and **sledding** in winter *(see page 76)*. However, you don't have to go in search of snow to ski or snowboard; Der Gletscher (The Glacier) ski centre in Pankow has the longest indoor ski course in the world.

Cycling through the Brandenburg Gate

Roller skating has become a way of life in Berlin; every Sunday evening – weather permitting – up to 4,000 skaters take part in a two-hour skate through the streets and squares of the city centre.

The most pleasant and effective defence against the aggressiveness of some of the city's **bicycle** riders is to rent a bike yourself. In the Tiergarten, meanwhile, **joggers** and roller skaters maintain a relationship of mutual disrespect.

Spectator Sports

The ultimate in professional football was seen when Berlin hosted the final of the football **World Cup** in 2006, for which the Olympic Stadium had undergone a massive programme of refurbishment *(see page 71)*. The annual **Six Day Cycle Race** has been held every January since 1997 at the Velodrom, while the Max-Schmeling-Halle draws **basketball** fans by the thousands to see the home team, Alba Berlin, take on the opposition. International **tennis** tournaments are held at the Rot-Weiß Club. **'Trotter' horse races** are held at two sites, and last, but by no means least, the **Berlin Marathon** can be enjoyed from the sidelines throughout the city every September.

Hertha Berlin

The Olympic Stadium is the home ground of Berlin's top football club, Hertha Berlin. Not as well known as clubs like Bayern Munich, it nevertheless enjoys moderate success in the Bundesliga and Europe.

CHILDREN'S BERLIN

Children are well catered for in Berlin, and many of the things you'll want to do – trips out to the Grunewald, city tours by canal – will also appeal to young ones.

Museums: Some of the city's museums are specifically intended for children, among them the **Kindermuseum 'Labyrinth'** with a whole range of interactive features, the **MachMit Museum** and the **Juniormuseum** of the **Ethnological Museum**. Other museums with definite child-appeal include the **Museum für Naturkunde** with its amazing dinosaur skeleton, the **Puppentheater-Museum** offering behind-the-scenes experience of puppets and marionettes, and the **Deutsches Technikmuseum**, especially the hands-on Spectrum section. At the **Domäne Dahlem** there are craftspeople to watch and animals to admire, while the **Mus-**

eumsdorf Düppel is a re-creation of a medieval village, also with craft and farming activities. There are animals aplenty in Berlin's two zoos, the Zoologischer Garten near the Ku'-damm and the Tierpark in Friedrichsfelde.

Parks and play areas: Well-equipped and -maintained play areas can be found all over the city, in local neighbourhoods and in the many parks. The finest is probably the **Britzer Garten** in Neukölln, with all the usual features plus pools, water playground, animals and a miniature railway. On rainy days you could try the more commercial **Jacks Fun World** (in Reinickendorf), which has go-karts, bungee-trampoline, bumper-boats and more.

Filmpark Babelsberg

Other attractions: Loxx Miniatur Welten, the world's largest digitally controlled model railway, puts the capital into miniature perspective (Meinekestraße, Charlottenburg). There's a Planetarium (Prenzlauer Allee 80, Prenzlauer Berg), an impressive AquaDom and Sea Life Centre (Spandauer Straße 3, Mitte), while the Ufa-Fabrik (Viktoriastraße 13–18, Tempelhof) has a children's circus and a farmyard. The Blue Man Group, housed in the former IMAX cinema, appeals to older kids as well as their parents. On the way to Potsdam, the **Filmpark Babelsberg** will easily keep the family busy for a whole day.

Calendar of Events

For the most up-to-date information on the city's festivals and arts calendar, consult the tourist office, the monthly *Berlin Programm* or the local press. The following list gives a flavour of some of the major events.

January: *Berliner Neujahrslauf:* A 4km (2.4-mile) run through the city streets, starting at the Brandenburg Gate; *Sechs-Tage-Rennen:* Six-day cycle race at the Velodrom; *Internationale Grüne Woche:* Food and agriculture fair, with specialities from around the world.

February: *Internationale Filmfestspiele Berlin:* Berlin's International Film Festival, in early February, rivals those in Cannes and Venice.

March/April: *Festtage* (classical music festival around Easter holidays): Staatsoper Unter den Linden.

May: *Theatertreffen:* A German-language theatre festival with productions from all over Germany, Austria and Switzerland. *Karneval der Kulturen:* Three days of multi-cultural song and dance on the streets of Kreuzberg.

May–Sept: *MuseumsInselFestival:* Nightly events (film, concerts, theatre) on three stages at the Museumsinsel, Kulturforum and Museen Dahlem.

June: Open-air classical music concerts by the Berlin Philharmonic at the Waldbühne. *Christopher Street Day:* Largest gay and lesbian event of its kind in Europe, with markets, food, performances.

July/August: Lots of open-air festivals throughout the city, from the beer-festival to the Köpenicker-Blues & Jazzfestival.

September/October: *Berlin Marathon; Musikfest Berlin:* A major international festival of orchestra and chamber music. *Internationales Stadionfest (ISTAF):* The Olympic Stadium plays host to a major international track and field event.

October/November: *Tag der Deutschen Einheit:* (3 October) Celebrations, including a big parade, to commemorate German reunification; *Oktoberfest:* Beer and food festival. *JazzFest Berlin:* A festival featuring both mainstream and avant-garde jazz.

December: *Winterzauber,* including *Weihnachtsmarkt:* Traditional Christmas markets are held on Breitscheidplatz and throughout the city. New Year's Eve party at the Brandenburg Gate.

EATING OUT

Berlin has a greater variety of cuisine than any other German city, offering anything from Japanese, Hungarian, Italian and Czech to Arabic, Turkish and Indonesian. A new German cuisine *(neue deutsche Küche)* has also emerged in response to a demand for greater culinary refinement. It doesn't mean that good old German dishes are being replaced by French imitations, but more and more they are being prepared with a new delicacy and imagination.

When to Eat

Mealtimes are quite flexible in Berlin, and you can always find something to eat somewhere at virtually any time of day or night. Breakfast *(Frühstück)* is the most important meal of the day, and generally consists of a selection of rolls, boiled eggs, cheese, muesli and honey, cold meats, fruit juices, *Quark* (soft cheese), yoghurt, and either coffee or tea. In hotels it can be served from as early as 6am until 11am, while many cafés offer a selection of breakfasts from about 9 or 10am until as late as 6pm.

A popular tradition in many eating places is the morning buffet, *Frühstücksbuffet*, where you help yourself from the counter to as much as you can eat for a fixed price. Berliners take lunch *(Mittagessen)* less seriously than other Germans, probably because the presence of so many fast-food *(Imbiss)* places leads to constant snacking. In the evening, restaurants tend to fill up early and you should reserve in advance for the better establishments.

Where to Eat

Choices range from high-class *Restaurants* and bourgeois *Gaststätten* via the rather chic and arty *Bistro* or *Café* down to the popular *Kneipe*, originally student slang for any corner bar or tavern where you can have a drink and a snack big enough to call a meal. All of these places spill out onto the streets and squares as soon as the weather is warm enough; when it is not, there are outdoor heaters.

The *Konditorei* (café-cum-pastry shop) is in a separate category all of its own. In this bourgeois paradise, and armed with a newspaper attached to a rod, you can indulge in the great German tradition of *Kaffee und Kuchen*, enjoyed by all. As well as cakes and pastries, ice cream, coffee, tea, hot chocolate, fruit juices and even wines, most places also offer a few light snacks and salads to stave off the hunger pangs. With its raised outdoor terrace, the opulent Operncafé on Unter den Linden is perhaps the best place to sit and sample something from a huge daily selection of exquisite homemade cakes.

Inside the Operncafé on Unter den Linden

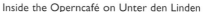

And don't forget the deli department on the sixth floor of KaDeWe, where you can sample a quite dazzling array of delicious foods from all around the world *(see also pages 35 and 93–4)*.

Cafés provide an excellent place just to sit and watch the world rush by while you relax. It's possible to order a cup of coffee and then sit for hours without feeling pressured to leave, but you can also dine extremely well in Berlin cafés for little expense.

Brauhaus (literally brewery) or *Bierkeller*, the old beer-halls, continue to thrive, and become *Biergarten* in the parks. You're always assured of good beer, hearty food and congenial company.

Al fresco at Hackescher Markt

A menu *(Speisekarte)* is displayed outside most restaurants. Besides the à la carte menu, there are generally one or more set menus *(Menü* or *Gedeck)*, which usually offer good value for money. The service charge *(Bedienung)* as well as value-added tax *(Mwst)* are usually included.

Soups and Starters

Appetisers (or starters) can be found listed on the menu under *Vorspeisen*, *Kleine Gerichte* or *Kalte Platten*. Soups *(Suppen)* and stews *(Eintopfgerichte)* are often very hearty; sometimes they can be enough for a whole meal. You can sample all the traditional German soups in Berlin. *Leberknödelsuppe* comes with spicy dumplings of flour, breadcrumbs, ox liver, onions, marjoram and garlic. Served at its best, *Kartoffelsuppe* is a rich combination of potato, leeks,

parsnips, celery and bacon, while *Bohnensuppe* is a hearty concoction of several varieties of beans. The city's favourite, however, is plain old lentil soup *(Linsensuppe)*, best with pieces of sausage in it.

The following two are typical starters: *Hackepeter*, the German version of steak tartare, and *Soleier*, eggs pickled in brine *(Sole)*, then peeled and halved and seasoned with salt, pepper, paprika, vinegar and oil. They are generally eaten with the ubiquitous Berlin mustard – *Mostrich*.

Main Dishes

Fish is served fresh from the River Havel. Try specialities like *Havelaal grün*, eel boiled in a dill sauce, or *Havelzander*, pike-perch served with *Salzkartoffeln*, simple (but surprisingly tasty) boiled potatoes. This very humble vegetable is something of a Berlin obsession. One of the city's great gourmet delights is the *Kartoffelpuffer*, a sort of potato pancake; *Kartoffelsalat* (potato salad) is also popular.

The supreme Berlin delicacy is undoubtedly *Eisbein mit Sauerkraut und Erbsenpüree* – pork knuckle on a purée of peas with sauerkraut prepared in white wine, juniper berries, caraway seeds and cloves. Add a generous dollop of mustard, as always. A little more humble, but just as fine, is *gebratene Leber*, also known as *Leber Berliner Art*, sautéed liver served with slices of apple and browned onion rings.

The original recipe for *Kasseler Rippen*, or smoked pork chops, came not from the town of Kassel, but from a Berlin butcher by the name of Kassel. Berlin also claims as its own two world-famous sausages: the giant *Bockwurst* (a type of boiled sausage), so named because a local butcher advertised it suspended between the mouths of two goats *(Bock)*; and the Viennese sausage, or *Wiener*, was invented, so they say, in Berlin.

In this predominantly meat-oriented culture, vegetarians may end up feeling rather excluded. The good news, however, is that a number of places are beginning to include vegetarian dishes on their menus. *Gemüsestrudel*, (a type of vegetable strudel) is made from courgettes, onions, sweetcorn, peppers and broccoli in a spicy tomato sauce, and wrapped in flaky pastry. *Ofenkartoffel mit Kräuterquark* (baked potato filled with herb-flavoured soft cheese) is also a filling standby. Be wary of ordering something which perhaps sounds as if it will be meat-free, for example potato or lentil soup, but which will often contain bacon *(Speck)* or sausage.

Desserts

A very popular dessert is *Rote Grütze* (a delicious compote of raspberries, cherries and blackcurrants), generally

Snacks

One of the first things you will probably notice about Berlin is its huge number of *Imbiß* (fast-food) stalls, offering a startling array of different foods. As well as serving *Boulette* (a kind of meatball) and *Currywurst* (sausage in a curry sauce), you can also find many ethnic fast-food outlets offering spicy samosas, lentil patties and, a great favourite, *Döner Kebap*.

Popular haunt on Oranienburger Straße

served with *Vanillesoße* (vanilla sauce). If you really want to stretch your waistline, indulge yourself in the German national orgy of Konditorei treats like *Schwarzwälder Kirschtorte*, the creamy cherry cake from the Black Forest; *Apfelstrudel* from Vienna, is another favourite dessert. Berliners also love *Haselnuss-Sahnetorte* (hazelnut cream cake), *Käsekuchen* (cheesecake) and *Pflaumenkuchen* (Dresden plum cake).

What to Drink

Frederick the Great tried to produce wine at Potsdam and the resulting brew was terrible, but today many Berlin restaurants offer a first-class array of many fine German wines. The red wines cannot be compared in quality to the famous white Rieslings of the Rhine and Mosel valleys but, generally speaking, the whole family of German wines is very respectable.

The most highly regarded German wines are those of the Rheingau. Among the labels to look for are Schloss Johannisberger, Hattenheimer, Kloster Eberbacher, Steinberger and Rüdesheimer. If you feel like celebrating, you won't go wrong with a bottle of the champagne-like Sekt. The best of the Rhine Valley red wines come from Assmannshausen and Ingelheim. From Rheinhessen, try the great Niersteiner Domtal and Oppenheimer. Bottled in green glass to distinguish them from the brown Rhine bottles, the Mosel wines enjoy their own delicate reputation. The most celebrated among the varietals include the Bernkasteler, Piesporter, Graacher and the Zeltinger.

Berlin's most popular drink, however, is still beer – local Schultheiss and Kindl, or the best Dortmund and Bavarian brews. They are served *vom Fass*, on tap, or bottled in several varieties: *Export*, light and smooth; *Pils*, light and

Outdoor tables on the Ku'damm

strong; and *Bock*, which is
dark and rich.

In the summer months, as
a refreshing surprise, try the
Berliner Weiße, a foaming
draught beer served up in a
huge bowl-like glass com-
plete with a shot of rasp-
berry syrup or liqueur, or
perhaps with *Waldmeister*
(green woodruff syrup).

Berliners also like the custom of 'chasing' the beer
with a shot of Schnapps –
any hard, clear alcohol made
from potatoes, corn, barley,

Gourmet delights

juniper, or another grain or berry that will distil into something to warm the cockles of your heart; a nice treat during
the winter months.

Brandy *(Weinbrand)* made in Germany is quite good, but
the very strong fruit Schnapps which are distilled either from
cherries *(Kirschwasser)*, plums *(Zwetschgenwasser)* or raspberries *(Himbeergeist)* are much better.

No matter what your 'poison', *Prost*!

Table Manners

On one or two of the long tables in the beer halls *(Bierkeller)* or other big restaurants, you will occasionally see a
sign proclaiming *Stammtisch*, which means a table for reg-
ulars; the custom dates back to the medieval craft guilds.
It is otherwise customary for strangers to sit together, usually after a polite inquiry as to whether one of the empty
places is *'frei'*. As they sit down they wish each other *'Mahl-
zeit'* or *'Guten Appetit'*.

HANDY TRAVEL TIPS

An A–Z Summary of Practical Information

A

ACCOMMODATION (see also CAMPING on page 108, and RECOMMENDED HOTELS on page 128)

The Berlin Tourist Office publishes an English/German language list with full details of accommodation, ranging from the most expensive hotels to small guesthouses. The office also provides a reservation service, tel: 25 00 25; fax: 25 00 24 24; or contact them via the internet at <www.berlin-tourist-information.de>. You can also inquire at the BERLIN infostores at the Europa-Center, Brandenburg Gate, Reichstag, Alexanderplatz, Hauptbahnhof or Tegel Airport (see pages 125–6). It is always advisable to book at least a month ahead.

I'd like a single/double room	**Ich möchte bitte ein Einzel-/ Doppelzimmer.**
with bath/shower	**mit Bad/Dusche**
What's the rate per night?	**Wieviel kostet es pro Nacht?**

AIRPORTS (Flughafen)

Berlin-Tegel, the gateway to Western Europe and New York, lies 8km (5 miles) northwest of the city centre. The best way into town is by express bus X9 to the bus station in front of Zoologischer Garten station or by express bus TXL to Unter den Linden and Alexanderplatz. Buses leave regularly. Two local buses call at U-Bahn stations, enabling you to continue your journey by underground train to any part of the city: number 109 to Zoologischer Garten stops at U-Bahn Jakob-Kaiser-Platz (two stops from the airport), and number 128 to Osloer Straße stops at U-Bahn Kurt-Schumacher-Platz (five stops from the airport).

Schönefeld Airport, which is mainly used for holiday flights, low-budget flights with airlines like easyJet and Ryanair, and flights to

Eastern Europe and Asia, lies about 19km (12 miles) southeast of the city centre and is served by S-Bahn. Lines S9 and S45 will take you to Alexanderplatz, from where bus, U- and S-Bahn connections to the rest of the city are plentiful. There is also the ExpressBus X7, connecting the airport with the underground station U Rudow (U-Bahn line 7).

Tempelhof Airport, the smallest airport, is very centrally located and linked to the city centre by the underground line 6.

Airport information. One telephone number covers information for all of the airports, tel: 0180 5000 186.

Where can I get a taxi?	**Wo finde ich ein Taxi?**
How much is it to the centre/ Potsdamer Platz?	**Wieviel kostet es ins Zentrum/ zum Potsdamer Platz?**
Does this bus go to the Ku'damm?	**Fährt dieser Bus zum Ku'damm?**

B

BICYCLE HIRE (Fahrradverleih)

Berlin's cyclists are relatively safe from the traffic in their own special network of bicycle lanes. These are usually marked by red bricks between the pavement and the road. Pedestrians should take special care to avoid walking in these lanes, especially as few cycles seem to possess warning bells. Bikes are easy to rent; either look in the *Gelbe Seiten* (Yellow Pages) under *Fahrradverleih*, or call 0180 510 8000 for information, or contact one of the following: Fahrradstation, Friedrichstraße 95 (entrance Dorotheenstraße 30), tel: 20 45 45 66, open Mon–Fri 8am–8pm, Sat 9am–5pm, Sun 9am–2pm.

Fahrradstation, Auguststraße 29, tel: 28 59 96 61, open Mon–Fri 10am–7pm and Sat 10am–3pm.

Fahrradstation, Bergmannstraße 9, tel: 215 15 66, open Mon–Fri 10am–7pm and Sat 10am–4pm.

German Railways (DB) have also introduced a bike hire scheme, tel: 0700 05 22 55 22.

BUDGETING FOR YOUR TRIP

The following list will give you some idea of what prices to expect in Berlin, but it can only be considered approximate as costs can change regularly. The sales tax (normally included) is 19 percent.

Welcome Card. There are a number of discount programmes available, which are worth taking advantage of. The Welcome Card (€24 for 72 hours, €17.50 for 48 hours) offers an excellent way of making significant savings on public transport costs, while providing reductions of up to 50 percent in entry prices for many of the city's major museums and attractions. Holders of valid cards, which are available from the Tourist Offices, S-Bahn ticket offices, BVG ticket offices and many hotels, are entitled to unlimited use of all buses and trains of the Berlin–Brandenburg public transport network.

Airport transfer. S-Bahn (suburban train) from Schönefeld €2.70, taxi from Tegel to Mitte €20, from Schönefeld €30.

Babysitters. €7–10 per hour.

Camping. *Tent:* €5–10 per person per night; *caravan (trailer):* €12 per person per night.

Car rental. *VW Polo:* €40 per day, *BMW3:* €75 per day.

Entertainment. *Cinema:* €4.50–10, *theatre:* €11–38, *club:* €3–15.

Hotels (double room per night). Luxury class €250–450, first class €150–250, medium range €80–150, budget class €40–80.

Meals and drinks. Breakfast €5–20, lunch or dinner in fairly good establishment €20–45, bottle of wine (German) €20–30, beer (half-litre) €3–4, soft drink (small bottle) €2–3, coffee €1.50–2.90.

Museums. Generally around €4–8, with reductions for students and free entrance to state museums for children under 16. The three-day museum tourist ticket or *Schaulustkarte* (€15) offers admission to the museums on Museumsinsel, together with around 50 other museums in Berlin. Tickets are available from the Tourist Offices and museums.

C

CAMPING

Campingplatz Am Krossinsee, Wernsdorfer Straße 38, Köpenick, Berlin, tel: 675 86 87.

Campingplatz Breitehorn, Breitehornweg 24, Spandau, Berlin, tel: 365 34 08.

Campingplatz Bürgerablage, Niederneuendorfer Allee, Spandau, Berlin, tel: 335 45 84.

Campingplatz Kladow, Krampnitzer Weg 111–117, Spandau, Berlin, tel: 365 27 97.

Tentstation Berlin, Seydlitzstraße 6, Mitte, tel: 39 40 46 50, <www.tentstation.de>.

WohnmobilPark Berlin, Waidmannsluster Damm 12–14, Tegel, tel: 20 16 63 33, <www.stellplatz-berlin.de>.

For full information about campsites, consult the guides published by the German Automobile Club, ADAC, <www.adac.de>.

CAR HIRE (See also DRIVING)

The best way to hire a car is through the internet before you leave home. You can also arrange to hire a car immediately upon arrival at Tegel or Schönefeld airports with one of the major international companies. Otherwise inquire at your hotel or refer to the yellow pages of the telephone directory under *Autovermietung* for addresses of leading companies.

To hire a car you'll need a valid driving licence held for at least one year and a credit card. The minimum age is 19, although some companies may have a higher minimum age.

I'd like to rent a car	Ich möchte bitte ein Auto mieten
tomorrow	für morgen
for one day/week	für einen Tag/für eine Woche
Please include	Bitte schließen Sie eine
full insurance.	Vollkaskoversicherung ab.

CLIMATE

Berlin's climate follows the continental pattern of cold, snowy winters and agreeably warm summers with low humidity. The best time for a visit is late spring or summer when temperatures tend to be mild. Average temperatures are as follows:

	J	F	M	A	M	J	J	A	S	O	N	D
°C max	2	3	8	13	19	22	25	23	20	13	7	3
°C min	-3	-3	0	4	8	12	14	13	10	6	2	-1
°F max	35	37	46	56	66	72	75	74	68	56	45	38
°F min	26	26	31	39	47	53	57	56	50	42	36	29

CLOTHING

Pack clothing for the season: heavy coat in winter, light garments and swimwear in summer, raincoat and sweater in spring and autumn.

CRIME AND THEFT

Like most urban centres, Berlin's crime rate is, unfortunately, on the increase. Leave valuables in the hotel safe. Be wary of pickpockets in crowds, do not wear conspicuous jewellery, and don't leave objects unattended in a parked car. Report an incident to your hotel and the nearest police station. The police will give you a certificate to present to your insurance company, or to your consulate if your passport has been stolen. It's wise to make photocopies of important documents such as your passport and plane tickets.

CUSTOMS *(Zoll)* AND ENTRY REQUIREMENTS

Visitors from EU countries only need an identity card (or passport) to enter Germany. Citizens of most other countries, including the US, Canada, Australia and New Zealand, must have a valid passport. European and North American residents are not subject to any health requirements. In case of doubt, check with German representatives in your own country before departure.

As Germany is a member of the European Union (EU), free exchange of non-duty-free goods for personal use is permitted between Germany and the UK and Ireland.

Currency restrictions. There is no limit on the amount of euros or other currency that can be brought into or taken out of the country by non-residents.

| I have nothing to declare. | **Ich habe nichts zu verzollen.** |

D

DRIVING

To enter Germany with your car you will need the following: a national driving licence (or an international licence for those coming from the US, Australia, New Zealand and South Africa); car registration papers; a national identity sticker for your car; a red warning triangle in case of breakdown; and a first-aid kit.

Insurance. Third-party insurance is compulsory. Visitors from abroad, except those from EU and certain other European countries, will have to present their international certificate (Green Card) or take out third-party insurance at the border.

Driving conditions. Rush-hour traffic jams and lack of parking space make driving in central Berlin somewhat frustrating. At the beginning and end of peak holiday periods, bottlenecks tend to form on approach roads into Berlin, but traffic generally flows.

Drive on the right, pass on the left. Seat belts are obligatory. If you don't wear your seat belt, insurance companies reduce compensation in the event of an accident, and you can be fined by the police.

Speed limits. The speed limit in Germany is 100km/h (60mph) on all open roads except motorways and divided highways, where there's no limit unless indicated. (The suggested maximum speed is 130km/h, or 80mph.) In town, speed is restricted to 50km/h (30mph), and often 30km/h (20mph). Cars with trailers may not exceed 80km/h (50mph).

Traffic police may confiscate the car keys of persons they consider unfit to drive. The permissible blood-alcohol level is 0.5 mg per ml.

Breakdowns. For round-the-clock breakdown service call ADAC Auto Assistance, tel: 01802 22 22 22.

Fuel and oil *(Benzin; Öl)*. You'll find petrol stations everywhere, most of them self-service. Many are open 24 hours.

Einbahnstraße	one-way street
Einordnen	get into lane
Fußgänger	pedestrians
Kurzparkzone	short-term parking
Rechts fahren	keep right
Parken verboten	no parking
Umleitung	detour
Vorsicht	caution
driving licence	**Führerschein**
car registration papers	**Kraftfahrzeugpapiere**
green (insurance) card	**Grüne Versicherungskarte**

E

ELECTRICITY

Germany has 220–250 volt, 50-cycle AC. Plugs are the standard continental type, so British and North American devices will need an adaptor.

I need an adaptor/ a battery, please.	**Ich brauche bitte eine Adapter/ eine Batterie.**

EMAIL AND INTERNET SERVICES

Many hotels offer e-mail facilities to their guests. In addition, there are numerous internet cafés in the city. Their numbers are increasing all the time, but some convenient ones include:

Alpha Internet Café, Dunckerstr. 72. Open daily 3pm to midnight.
easyInternetcafé, Kurfürstendamm 224. Open daily 6.30am–2am.
Internet-Terminal, Kantstraße 38, Charlottenburg.
There are also many places where you can use wireless LAN.

EMBASSIES AND CONSULATES *(Botschaft; Konsulat)*

Get in touch with the consulate of your home country if you lose your passport, get into trouble with the authorities or the police, or have an accident. They can issue emergency passports, give advice on obtaining money from home and provide a list of lawyers, interpreters and doctors. It is advisable to phone in advance to check opening hours.

Australia: Wallstraße 76–79, 10179 Berlin, tel: 88 00 88-0.
Canada: Leipziger Platz 17, 10117 Berlin, tel: 20 31 20.
Ireland: Friedrichstraße 200, 10117 Berlin, tel: 22 07 20.
South Africa: Tiergartenstraße 18, 10785 Berlin, tel: 22 07 30.
UK: Wilhelmstraße 70–71, 10117 Berlin, tel: 20 45 70.
US: Neustädtische Kirchstraße 4–5, 10117 Berlin, tel: 830 50.

EMERGENCIES *(See also POLICE on page 120, and CRIME AND THEFT on page 109)*

The following emergency services are available 24 hours:

Police	**110**	Fire	**112**
Ambulance	**112**	Pharmacies	**0 11 41**
Medical assistance	**31 00 31**	AIDS Hotline	**194 11**

I need a doctor	**Ich brauche einen Doktor**
an ambulance	**einen Krankenwagen**
a hospital	**ein Krankenhaus**

ETIQUETTE

It is customary to shake hands when you meet someone in Germany, and to say '*Guten Tag*' on entering a shop and '*Auf Wiedersehen*' when leaving. '*Tschüß*' is a more familiar way of saying goodbye. When taking leave of someone on the telephone, you should say '*Auf Wiederhören*', literally, 'Until we hear each other again'. The word for 'please' is '*bitte*', also used in the sense of 'you're welcome', and 'thank you' is '*Danke schön*'.

G

GAY AND LESBIAN TRAVELLERS

Berlin has a thriving gay culture. In the 1920s, the city became one of the first in the world to have a widely recognised gay community. Although Nazi persecution resulted in many homosexuals being interned in concentration camps, where some 100,000 died, gay life re-established itself post-war. Homosexuals were more tolerated in West than East Berlin but, since reunification, acceptance is far more general across the city, and there is a massive celebration of gay culture every year with the lesbian/gay street festival in early June at Nollendorfplatz and the Christopher Street Day Parade in late June.

The Schwules Museum (Mehringdamm 61, Kreuzberg) has a large collection of documents and artworks related to the history of gay and lesbian movements.

For information about ongoing events and related links visit <http://berlin.gay-web.de>.

GETTING TO BERLIN

By air. There are direct daily flights to Berlin from major airports all over Europe, though travel from the US (except New York) often requires a change of planes in Frankfurt or other European city. The cheapest fares on regular flights are available through internet retailers, particularly if you book well in advance. However, if you want a more flexible ticket, talk to a reliable travel agent. Some carriers have a special round-trip fare that can be ticketed at any time, and some of the 'budget' airlines, such as Ryanair and easyJet, offer very low fares, although you may only have a limited choice of flight times. Unless you leave things until the last minute, you should be able to book a charter flight or package including hotel, for a good rate.

By rail. There are direct rail services between Berlin and numerous major European cities, including Amsterdam, Paris and Prague. Trains to Brussels connect with Eurostar services which use the Channel Tunnel and continue to London Waterloo. The main station in Berlin is the Hauptbahnhof.

Deutsche Bahn (German Rail) trains are extremely comfortable and fast and normally punctual. EC (EuroCity) are international trains; IC (InterCity) and ICE (Inter City Express) are long-distance national trains. The ICE trains are very fast, reaching speeds of up to 280km/h (174mph), and feature restaurants and aircraft-like video screens on some seats. First-class travel on the Deutsche Bahn costs double the second-class fare. A supplement is charged for travel on EuroCity, ICE and InterCity trains. Children under 4 travel free in Germany, 4 to 12 year-olds pay half fare.

There are several 'go-as-you-please' passes. They include: Eurail passes (these rover tickets covering Western Europe are only available to those living outside Europe, and must be bought before you arrive in Europe); the German Rail pass, which allows unlimited travel in Germany for any three to eight days within one month, and the Bahncard – suitable for frequent travellers in Germany, this allows discounts of 25 or 50 percent off the regular fare for all train journeys in the country over a one-year period. Detailed information is available, in English, from the International Visitors section of the Deutsche Bahn website <www.bahn.de> or by calling the Deutsche Bahn UK Booking Centre in England, tel: (+44) 0870 2435363.

By road. From the UK the Harwich/Cuxhaven crossing takes 21 hours and brings you closer to Berlin (415km/258 miles) than crossings from the British Channel ports do.

GUIDES AND TOURS

The tourist office (BTM) will put you in touch with qualified guides and interpreters for personally conducted tours.

City sightseeing tours by bus are an excellent introduction to Berlin, and most companies offer multilingual recorded commentary. Daily excursions by coach to Potsdam and the Spreewald are also available, as are weekend trips to other places in Germany, including Dresden and Wittenberg. Some companies also offer nightclub tours, and the price includes a drink and entry to a show.

Most sightseeing tours depart from the Kurfürstendamm, between Rankestraße and Fasanenstraße:

Berliner Bären Stadtrundfahrt (BBS), tel: 351 952 70. Departs from the Ku'damm at Rankestraße.

City-Circle-Tour (Berolina and BVB) departs Ku'damm at Meineckestraße every 15 minutes. You can leave and board the bus at 15 stops.

Top Tour (BVG-Stadtrouristik, tel: 256 255 69). Departs from Kurfürstendamm at Café Kranzler every 25 minutes. Visitors can hop

on or hop off where and when they wish. The day-pass is valid between 10am and 6pm.

Videobustour (Unter den Linden 40, tel: 44 02 44 50, <www.video
bustour.de>). Film, photos and sound material make this time-
travel shuttle an inspiring adventure in history.

Viewing Berlin from the River Spree and the city's canals is a fascinating experience. There's a wide choice of shorter or longer trips,
departing from a number of locations including the Nikolaiviertel
and Charlottenburger Ufer (near Schloss Charlottenburg).

Reederei Bruno Winkler, tel: 349 95 95

Stern und Kreis Schiffahrt, tel: 536 36 00

There are also a number of very good walking tour operators in
the city, the best of which are:

Berlin Walks, tel 301 91 94, which offers a choice of tours ranging from The Original Discover Berlin tour to Jewish Life in Berlin,
<www.berlinwalks.com>.

Insider Tour, tel: 692 31 49, whose guides are all native English
speakers, <www.insidertour.com>.

We'd like an English-speaking guide.	**Wir möchten bitte einen englisch-sprechenden Führer**
I'd like an English interpreter.	**Ich möchte bitte einen Dolmetscher**

LANGUAGE

Although you can expect many of the people you meet in the west
of the city to speak English, this will not necessarily be the case in
the east, and a little German will go a long way towards breaking
the ice. The *Berlitz German Phrase Book & Dictionary* covers most
of the situations you are likely to encounter in Germany, and the
German–English/English–German pocket dictionary contains a special menu-reader supplement and a short grammar section.

LAUNDRY AND DRY CLEANING

Having your laundry washed or cleaned by the hotel is the quickest and most convenient method, but prices are high. Seek out a *Waschsalon* (launderette) or *Wäscherei* (laundry). Dry cleaning usually takes two days. Some cleaners offer a quick service *(Schnellreinigung)* which takes a minimum of two hours and is slightly more expensive.

LOST PROPERTY

Berlin's central lost-property office *(Zentrales Fundbüro)* is at Platz der Luftbrücke 6 (Tempelhof), tel: 7560-3101. Open Mon–Tues 8am–3pm, Thur 1–6pm, Fri 8am–noon.

If you think you know where you left your property, call the *Fundbüro* of the service concerned. If it was on public transport, contact the BVG at Potsdamerstraße 180–182 (Schöneberg), tel: 19 449.

M

MAPS

Excellent free street maps *(Stadtplan)* are available at the tourist offices, some car hire agencies and larger hotels.

MEDICAL CARE

Ask your insurance company before leaving home if you are covered for medical treatment in Germany. Visitors who are not reimbursed for medical bills abroad can take out a short-term holiday policy before leaving. Citizens of EU countries may use the German Health Services for medical treatment on presentation of a European Health Insurance Card. This can be applied for at post offices in the UK and Ireland.

In the event of accident or serious illness, call for an ambulance, **112**, or ask the medical emergency service, tel: **31 00 31**, to recommend a doctor.

Pharmacies are open during normal shopping hours. At night and on Sundays and holidays, all pharmacies display the address of the nearest one open. Berlin has a special telephone sevice, Call a Doc, tel: 01804 22 55 23 62, <www.calladoc.com>. You can also find health information at <www.gesundheit-info.de>.

Where's the nearest (all-night) pharmacy?	**Wo ist die nächste Apotheke (mit Nachtdienst)?**

MONEY MATTERS

Currency. In common with most other EU countries, the euro (EUR) is the official currency used in Germany. Notes are denominated in 5, 10, 20, 50, 100 and 500 euros; coins in 1 and 2 euros and 1, 2, 5, 10, 20 and 50 cents.

Banking hours are usually 9am–3pm Mon–Fri. Most banks remain open one or more afternoons a week; however days vary, so you'll have to check posted notices. The currency exchange office of the ReiseBank in the Hauptbahnhof is open 8am–10pm

Can I pay with this credit card?	**Kann ich mit dieser Kreditkarte bezahlen?**
I want to change some pounds/dollars.	**Ich möchte Pfund/Dollar wechseln.**
Can you cash a traveller's cheque?	**Können sie einen Reisescheck einlösen?**
Where's the nearest bank/ currency exchange office?	**Wo ist die nächste Bank/ Wechselstube?**
Is there a cash machine near here?	**Gibt es hier einen Geldautomaten?**
How much is that?	**Wieviel kostet das?**

daily and there are branches at Bahnhof Friedrichstraße and Bahnhof Zoo.

Changing money. The easiest way to obtain euros is with a debit/ credit card at an ATM machine. Foreign currency can be changed at ordinary banks *(Bank)*, savings banks *(Sparkasse)*, and currency exchange offices *(Wechselstube)*. Hotels, travel agencies, and the central post office also have exchange facilities, but rates are less favourable.

Credit cards are accepted in most hotels, restaurants and large shops.

NEWSPAPERS AND MAGAZINES *(Zeitungen; Zeitschriften)*

Major American, British and other European newspapers and magazines are on sale at newsagents and kiosks in the city centre, as well as at big hotels and at the airports.

O

OPENING HOURS

Department stores are open between 10am and 8pm on weekdays and Saturdays. Smaller shops may not open until around 10am and close early on Saturday.

Most museums in Berlin are closed on Monday; for opening times check the individual entries in the Where to Go section. For opening times of banks *see page 118*.

P

PHOTOGRAPHY AND VIDEO

All makes of film are easily found and can be developed overnight or within an hour. Digital accessories and video cassettes are also widely available, though you must make sure they are compatible with your equipment back home.

POLICE *(Polizei)*

Germany's police officers wear green uniforms (soon to be blue). You'll see them on white motorcycles or in green-and-white (soon to be blue-and-grey) cars or vans. The police emergency number is **110**.

Where's the nearest police station?	**Wo ist die nächste Polizeistation?**
I've lost my... wallet/bag/passport.	**Ich habe... meine Brieftasche/meine Tasche/ meinen Reisepass verloren.**

POST OFFICES

Postboxes are bright yellow and, if there is more than one slot on a mail box, you should deposit non-local letters or cards in the slot marked *Andere PLZ*.

Telegrams, packages, money orders and registered mail can be sent from post offices. Stamps and pre-paid telephone cards are sold there in various denominations.

The post office at Flughafen Tegel (airport) is open from 8am–6pm Monday–Friday, and 8am–1pm on Saturday. The self-service area is open 24 hours. The branch at Potsdamer Platz Arkaden is open 10am–8pm Monday–Friday, 10am–4pm on Saturday, and also has 24-hour self-service area. Information on other postal services can be found at: <www.deutschepost.de>.

Where's the nearest post office?	**Wo ist das nächste Postamt?**
express (special delivery)	**per Eilboten**
registered	**per Einschreiben**

PUBLIC HOLIDAYS *(Feiertag)*

The chart below shows the public holidays celebrated in Berlin when shops, banks, official departments and many restaurants are closed. If a holiday falls on a Thursday, many people take the Friday off to make a long weekend.

Note that on 24 December (Christmas Eve), shops stay open until noon, but most restaurants, theatres, cinemas and concert halls are closed.

1 January	**Neujahr**	New Year's Day
1 May	**Tag der Arbeit**	Labour Day
3 October	**Nationalfeiertag**	Reunification Day
25, 26 December	**Weihnachten**	Christmas
Movable dates:	**Karfreitag**	Good Friday
	Ostermontag	Easter Monday
	Christi Himmelfahrt	Ascension Day
	Pfingstmontag	Whit Monday

PUBLIC TRANSPORT

Berlin is served by an efficient network of buses, trams, U-Bahn (underground railway), S-Bahn (suburban railway), and Regionalbahn (regional railway), administered by the *Berliner Verkehrsbetriebe*, or BVG for short. The U-Bahn currently covers the inner city and many outlying districts, while the bus service reaches nearly every corner of Berlin. The S-Bahn (administrated by Deutsche Bahn) provides an efficient link to places further afield such as the Grunewald, Wannsee, Potsdam and Köpenick, and its central, overhead section linking Savignyplatz, Zoologischer Garten, Friedrichstraße and Alexanderplatz is particularly useful. The tram network operates mainly in the former East Berlin.

The **U-Bahn** operates from about 4.30am to about 1am Sunday to Thursday; most lines run all night on Friday and Saturday. U-

Bahn stations are marked by a white 'U' on a blue background, and S-Bahn stations by a white 'S' on a green background.

Buses and **trams** run at least 20 hours a day at 10-minute intervals (every 20–30 minutes at night). Night bus routes coincide with the U-Bahn network. Bus stops are easily recognisable by a yellow sign marked with a green 'H'.

When's the next bus to ...?	**Wann geht der nächste Bus nach ...?**
Will you tell me when to get off?	**Könnten Sie mir bitte sagen, wann ich aussteigen muss.**

Tickets are interchangeable between trains, buses and trams, entitling you to free transfers for up to two hours (no return allowed). Be sure to have plenty of small change for the vending machines which distribute tickets at the U-Bahn stations and most bus stops. A few of them also take banknotes. If the machine rejects a coin try another (they tend to be unpredictable). Stamp your ticket at the start of your journey in one of the red or yellow machines (*Entwerter*) on station platforms and in buses. To buy a ticket on the bus itself, it's best to have the exact money ready, though drivers will give change. The most cost-effective option is to buy either a one-day ticket (*Tageskarte*), or a one-day group ticket (*Kleingruppenkarte*). They both allow travel up to 3am the day after the ticket is stamped at an *Entwerter*, and the group ticket covers up to five people. Holders of the Welcome Card, which is available from Tourist Offices for €24 (zones A, B, and C) or €21 (A and B), are

What's the fare to ... ?	**Wieviel kostet es nach ...?**
I want a ticket to ...	**Ich will eine Fahrkarte nach ...**
single/return	**einfache Karte/Rückfahrkarte**

entitled to 72 hours of unlimited use of public transport throughout the city, in addition to reduced entry prices for many of the city's major museums and attractions. A seven-day ticket (public transport only) costs €25.40 (A and B) or €31.30 (A, B and C).

Long-distance buses serve many destinations in Germany, departing from the central bus station (Zentral Omnibusbahnhof Funkturm, ZOB) near the Funkturm (radio tower) in Messedamm, tel: 302 53 61.

R

RADIO AND TV *(Radio, Fernsehen)*

It is easy to pick up the BBC World Service. As for television, there are two national channels – ARD and ZDF, plus a regional station, RBB, and several private and cable stations, while most hotels will also have satellite television, which will usually include CNN and BBC World.

RELIGION

A complete list of churches, synagogues, mosques and temples can be obtained from the tourist office *(see page 125)*.

Remember to always keep your head covered when in a synagogue or Jewish cemetery.

T

TAXIS

Berlin taxis are mostly cream-coloured Mercedes. Catch one at a stand, at busy locations such as the Ku'damm/Joachimstaler Straße intersection, or hail a driver. You can also book in advance through your hotel or by phoning, tel: 0800 222 22 55.

Where can I get a taxi?   **Wo finde ich ein Taxi?**

Velo Taxis are also available for those who would like to travel around the city in a bicycle-powered rickshaw. You may be able to hail one on the street, especially in busy tourist areas such as Ku'-damm, Unter den Linden and around the Brandenburg Gate (tel: 44 31 940; <www.velotaxi.com>).

TELEPHONES

The dialling code for Germany is 49. The dialling code for Berlin from outside the city is 030.

International calls can be made from phone booths, which will certainly be cheaper than phoning from your hotel room. Although some are still coin-operated, those accepting phone cards *(Telefonkarte)* are increasingly common, and there are some which also accept credit cards. Phone cards can be obtained at any post office and many kiosks. Communications within Germany and to neighbouring countries are cheaper from 6pm to 8am weekdays and all day Saturday and Sunday. Rates for Canada and the US are cut between midnight and noon.

Enquiries: domestic, tel: 11 8 33; international, tel: 11 8 34.

TIME DIFFERENCES

Germany follows Central European Time (GMT +1):

New York	London	**Berlin**	Jo'burg	Sydney	Auckland
6am	11am	**noon**	noon	8pm	10pm

TIPPING

Since a service charge is normally included in hotel and restaurant bills, tipping is not obligatory, although it is gladly accepted. It is appropriate to tip porters, taxi drivers, etc., for their services. See below for some suggestions as to how much you might want to leave.

Hairdresser/barber	10–15 percent
Lavatory attendant	€0.25–0.50

Maid, per week	€2.50–5.00
Porter, per bag	€0.50–1.00
Taxi driver	10 percent
Waiter	5–10 percent (optional)

TOILETS

Public toilets are readily found. Always have small coins ready in case the door has a coin slot. Toilets may be labelled with symbols of a man or a woman or the initials WC. Otherwise *Herren* (Gentlemen) or *Damen* (Ladies) are indicated.

Where are the toilets?   **Wo sind die Toiletten?**

TOURIST INFORMATION OFFICES

The headquarter of the German National Tourist Board – Deutsche Zentrale für Tourismus e.V. (DZT) – is located at: Beethovenstraße 69, D-60325 Frankfurt am Main, tel: (069) 97 46 40.

The German National Tourist Board also maintains offices in many countries throughout the world:

Canada: 480 University Avenue, Suite 1500, Toronto, Ontario M5G IV2, tel: (416) 968-1685.

UK: PO Box 2695, London W1A 3TN, tel: 020 7317 0908.

US: 122 East 42nd Street, New York, NY 10168-0072, tel: (212) 661-7200; 1334 Parkview Avenue, Suite 300, Manhattan Beach, CA 90266, tel: (310) 545-1350.

The Berlin Tourist Office – Berlin Tourismus Marketing GmbH (BTM) – is responsible for promoting and organising tourism in the city; their excellent website (<www.btm.de>; <www.berlin-tourist-information.de>) has up-to-date information on everything from accommodation to sightseeing, and provides online booking and ticket services. Information on hotels and tickets can also be obtained through their Berlin Hotline, tel: 25 00 25, fax: 25 00 24 24.

The BTM runs a number of **BERLIN infostores** in the city. To visit them online, click on 'Berlin Info' on the BTM home page.

Neues Kranzler Eck, Passage, Kurfürstendamm 21, Mon–Sat 10am–8pm, Sun 10am–6pm.

Brandenburger Tor, South Wing; daily 10am–7pm.

Hauptbahnhof (Central Station), Floor 0/Entrance North, Europa Platz 1; daily 8am–10pm.

Berlin Pavilion at Reichstag, Scheidemannstraße; daily 10am–6pm.

Some infostores operate longer opening hours Apr–Oct. There are also tourist information points at all three airports.

In addition to free maps, lists and brochures, Berlin's tourist offices sell the Welcome Card *(see page 107)* and museum tickets; tickets for the theatre and other events can also be purchased.

TRAVELLERS WITH DISABILITIES

Many efforts have been made to improve the city's accessibility to travellers with disabilities. Maps of the city transport network show which U- and S-Bahn stations have wheelchair facilities. Buses have wide rear doors and some have lifts and safety straps for wheelchairs. Several museums have wheelchair access, lifts, and specially adapted toilet facilities. *Berlin Programm* lists which of them cater to visitors with disabilities, although it is always best to phone in advance. For more information, contact the Berlin Tourist Office *(see above)*, or call one of the following associations:

Berliner Behinderten Verband e.V, tel: 204 38 47

Albatros e.V., tel: 7477 7115, <www.mobidat.net>.

W

WEBSITES

A great deal of information about Berlin can be obtained from the internet, and it's possible to book almost everything connected with your trip online. Some useful addresses are:

www.bahn.de – Deutsche Bahn website, with English-language section. It covers everything from train timetables to online bookings.

www.berlin.de – is the official internet site of the state of Berlin with service-oriented information and links for Berliners and visitors alike.

www.berlinonline.de – a slick, German-language website, with links to hotel and restaurant listings, museums, newspapers, events guides, etc.

www.berlin-tourist-information.de – BTM website, with extensive information on attractions and events. In German and English.

www.smb.museum – extremely useful site for all the state museums in Berlin. In German and English.

Y

YOUTH HOSTELS *(Jugendherberge)*

For information, contact the local branch of the German Youth Hostel Association (DJH Landesverband Berlin-Brandenburg) at Tempelhofer Ufer 32, 10963 Berlin, tel: 26 49 52-0. You can also reserve accommodation via their website: <www.djh-berlin-branden burg.de>. Youth hostels tend to get crowded, so you should always book ahead.

Berlin International, Kluckstr. 3, 10785 Berlin, tel: 261 10 98; fax: 265 03 83; e-mail: <jh-berlin@jugendherberge.de>.

Jugendgästehaus Am Wannsee, Badeweg 1, 14129 Berlin, tel: 803 20 34; fax: 803 59 08; e-mail: <jh-wannsee@jugendherberge.de>.

Jugendherberge Ernst Reuter, Hermsdorfer Damm 48–50, 13467 Berlin, tel: 404 16 10; fax: 404 59 72; e-mail: <jh-ernst-reuter@ jugendherberge.de>.

There is an increasing number of hostels for backpackers and single travellers from around the world. The A&O hostels are centrally located, have dormitories and private rooms, and friendly staff; <www.aohostels.com>.

Recommended Hotels

Below is a selection of hotels in four price categories, grouped in the following areas: Berlin City, west; Potsdamer Platz/Kreuzberg; Berlin City, east; Outskirts; and Potsdam. You are advised to book your accommodation well in advance.

Berlin has, as you'd expect from such a large city, a vast number of hotels, ranging from the most basic to luxurious establishments that rival the best in the world. In recent years, an increasing number of hotels have opened in former East Berlin, many of which are equal to or even surpass their western counterparts for elegance and facilities.

Breakfast is normally included in the price of the room, but some of the more expensive establishments ask for a supplementary charge. As a basic guide to prices, we have used the following symbols (for a double room with bath and usually breakfast):

€€€€	above €250
€€€	€250–150
€€	€80–150
€	below 80

The telephone country code for Germany is 49 and the city code for Berlin is 30.

BERLIN

BERLIN CITY, WEST

Artemisia Frauenhotel €€ *Brandenburgische Str. 18, 10707 Berlin, tel: 873 89 05, fax: 861 86 53, <www.frauenhotel-berlin. de>.* Berlin's pioneering women-only hotel. It also offers facilities for children. 12 rooms. Cosy sun deck.

Askanischer Hof €€€ *Kurfürstendamm 53, 10707 Berlin, tel: 881 80 33, fax: 881 72 06, <www.askanischer-hof.de>.* A small, family-run hotel in an excellent location. Delightful, authentic 1920s atmosphere and a very friendly reception. Children welcome. 16 rooms.

Astoria €€ *Fasanenstraße 2, 10623 Berlin, tel: 312 40 67, fax: 312 50 27, <www.hotelastoria.de>*. Very friendly hotel in a 19th-century town house in an agreeable central location just off the Kurfürstendamm. Special rates are available for children under 12. Babysitting facilities. 32 rooms.

Bristol-Hotel Kempinski €€€€ *Kurfürstendamm 27, 10719 Berlin, tel: 88 43 40, fax: 883 60 75, <www.kempinskiberlin. de>*. Large, luxurious hotel with excellent facilities: conference rooms, several restaurants, solarium, sauna, babysitting services, indoor swimming pool. The soundproofed rooms are extremely comfortable and pleasantly furnished. Disabled access. 301 rooms.

Designhotel Q! €€€ *Knesebeckstraße 67, 10623 Berlin, tel: 81 00 66-0, fax: 81 00 66-666, <www.loock-hotels.com>*. This establishment on the corner of the Ku'damm, takes the concept of the design hotel to its limits, with never a right angle in sight and a pervasive sense of playfulness. A unique experience. Very special bar.

The Ellington Hotel Berlin €€€–€€€€ *Nürnberger Straße 50–55, 10789 Berlin, tel: 68 31 50, fax: 68 31 55 555, <www. ellington-hotel.com>*. This hotel is housed in a magnificent building that conserves the architectural style of the golden twenties and offers high-quality, simple elegance, professional service and a lively atmosphere. It also hosts the world's biggest Elvis exhibition, from photographs and tie pins to his original stage costumes.

Grand Hotel Esplanade €€€–€€€€ *Lützowufer 15, 10785 Berlin, tel: 25 47 82 55, fax: 254 78 82 22, <www.esplanade.de>*. This recently renovated 'lifestyle' hotel features sleek and creative interior design. Harry's New-York Bar on the ground floor is one of the best addresses for long drinks in Berlin.

Hotel-Pension Funk €–€€ *Fasanenstraße 69, 10719 Berlin, tel: 882 71 93, fax: 883 33 29, <www.hotel-pensionfunk.de>*. This small hotel has comfortable rooms, though not all have showers. Located in one of the most delightful streets off the busy Kurfürstendamm, this art-nouveau building was once home to a silent screen star. 14 rooms.

Lindner Hotel am Ku'damm €€–€€€ *Kurfürstendamm 24, 10719 Berlin, tel: 818 25 0, fax: 818 25 25, <www.lindner.de>.* Part of the new City Quartier development at Kranzler Eck, the Lindner has comfortable and spacious rooms with state-of-the-art communications facilities. The Outlook restaurant, with its pleasant courtyard, has a variety of modern light food; there is a sauna and sun deck; and the Sky Club next door has a well-equipped gym. 146 rooms.

Mondial €€€ *Kurfürstendamm 47, 10707 Berlin, tel: 88 41 10, fax: 88 41 11 50, <www.hotel-mondial.com>.* Comfortable rooms and friendly service are just two of this hotel's assets. Excellent facilities for disabled visitors. Restaurant and bar, conference rooms, wellbeing area, and parking. 75 rooms.

NH Berlin Kurfürstendamm €€€ *Grolmanstraße 41–43, 10623 Berlin, tel: 88 42 60, fax: 88 42 65 00, <www.nh-hotels.com>.* In a quiet location near Savignyplatz, this elegant hotel offers tastefully furnished rooms, as well as a sauna and solarium, restaurant with garden terrace and bar. 167 rooms.

Schlossparkhotel €€€ *Heubnerweg 2a, 14059 Berlin, tel: 326 90 30, fax: 326 90 36 00.* Situated in a quiet location near Charlottenburg Palace gardens, the hotel offers a swimming pool as well as conference facilities. 32 rooms.

Hotel Seehof am Lietzensee €€€ *Lietzensee-Ufer 11, 14057 Berlin, tel: 32 00 20, fax: 32 00 22 51, <www.hotel-seehof-berlin. de>.* Modern hotel on the shores of a little lake in one of the city's most exclusive residential areas. There is a restaurant, swimming pool, solarium, sauna and Ayurveda treatments. The large rooms are traditionally decorated and many have wonderful views of the lake. 75 rooms.

POTSDAMER PLATZ/KREUZBERG

Berlin Marriott €€€–€€€€ *Inge-Beisheim-Platz 1, 10785 Berlin, tel: 22 00 00, fax: 22 00 01-000, <www.marriott.com>.* Part of the prestigious new Beisheim Center on Potsdamer Platz. Has all of the usual Marriott facilities. 379 rooms and suites, plus an executive floor.

Grand Hyatt Berlin €€€€ *Marlene-Dietrich-Platz 2, 10785 Berlin, tel: 25 53 12 34, fax: 25 53 12 35, <www.hyatt.de>.* Very modern hotel, located right on Potsdamer Platz, opposite the Musical Theatre. It is also within easy walking distance of the Kulturforum. Swimming pool, gym. Disabled access. 340 rooms.

Riehmers Hofgarten €€ *Yorckstraße 83, 10965 Berlin, tel: 78 09 88 00, fax: 78 09 88 08, <www.riehmers-hofgarten.de>.* Comfortable hotel in a charming historic building near leafy Viktoria Park, with restaurant and conference facilities. The hotel is excellently situated for exploring Kreuzberg and Mitte. 22 rooms.

Ritz-Carlton Berlin €€€€ *Potsdamer Platz 3, 10785 Berlin, tel: 33 77 77, fax: 33 77 75-555, <www.ritzcarlton.com/hotels/berlin>.* The ultimate in luxury occupying the main Chicago-style Beisheim Center building overlooking Potsdamer Platz. Interior design inspired by Karl Friedrich Schinkel. Excellent service. 302 rooms including luxury suites.

BERLIN CITY, EAST

Adlon Kempinski €€€€ *Unter den Linden 77, 10117 Berlin, tel: 22 61 11 11, fax: 22 61 22 22, <www.hotel-adlon.de>.* The original Hotel Adlon was a Berlin legend that welcomed such luminaries as Charlie Chaplin and Greta Garbo. It was destroyed in 1945. The new Adlon was built in 1997, and has remained true to the traditions of its famous predecessor, boasting the very best of everything in one of the world's top hotels, including a superb restaurant, Lorenz Adlon. The black marble elephant fountain in the hall once stood in the original Hotel Adlon. 336 rooms.

art'otel Berlin Mitte €€€ *Wallstraße 70–73; 10179 Berlin, tel: 24 06 20, fax: 24 06 22 22, <www.artotels.de>.* Elegant hotel with a mixture of classical and modern architecture and contemporary art and design. It has a stylish restaurant, the Factory. 109 rooms.

Hotel Hackescher Markt €€€ *Grosse Präsidentenstraße 8, 10178 Berlin, tel: 28 00 30, fax: 28 00 31 11, <www.loock-hotels. com>.* Elegant small modern hotel in a great location in one of eastern Berlin's trendiest quarters, with a wealth of bars, restaurants, shops and galleries all around. Many rooms face the quiet, leafy courtyard. Friendly reception. Wellbeing centre. 31 rooms.

Hilton Berlin €€€–€€€€ *Mohrenstraße 30, 10117 Berlin, tel: 20 23 0, fax: 20 23 42 69, <www.berlin.hilton.com>.* Modern hotel on the historic Gendarmenmarkt square. Offers excellent rooms as well as two restaurants, a bistro, a café, a bar and a pub. Sauna, swimming pool and squash court. Disabled access. 589 rooms.

Honigmond Pension €–€€ *Tieckstraße 12, 10243 Berlin, tel: 28 44 55-0, fax: 28 44 55 11, <www.honigmond.de>.* Fabulous pension, with large, beautifully appointed rooms, plus a bar and excellent restaurant. Friedrichstraße and Oranienburger Straße are within walking distance or a couple of stops by tram.

Hotel Luisenhof €€ *Köpenicker Straße 92, 10179 Berlin, tel: 241 59 06, fax: 279 29 83, <www.luisenhof.de>.* Situated in a charmingly restored 19th-century town house and ideally located for exploring the museums around Mitte. 27 rooms.

Hotel Märkischer Hof €–€€ *Linienstraße 133, 10115 Berlin, tel: 282 71 55, fax: 282 43 31, <www.maerkischer-hof-berlin.de>.* Conveniently located near Friedrichstraße, this recently-renovated, family-run hotel is welcoming and friendly, and the comfortable rooms are agreeably furnished. Services include conference facilities, TV, radio and telephone in all rooms, as well as a guest lounge. 20 rooms.

Park Inn Hotel Berlin €€–€€€ *Alexanderplatz, 10178 Berlin, tel: 23 890, fax: 23 89 43 05, <www.rezidorparkinn.com>.* The 37-

storey hotel offers stunning views from its rooms and elegant interiors, though the bedrooms are generally small. It also has a casino on the upper floor. 1,006 rooms.

Radisson SAS Hotel Berlin €€€ *Karl-Liebknecht-Straße 5, 10178 Berlin, tel: 23 82 80, fax: 238 28 10, <www.radissonsas. com>.* Modern hotel located close to the Berliner Dom and Museumsinsel. The hotel's lobby holds the world's largest cylindrical spectacular aquarium. Stocked with 2,500 exotic tropical fish, the AquaDom is 25 metres high and open to the public *(see page 90).* Facilities include four restaurants, sauna, conference centre, bar. 427 rooms.

The Regent €€€€ *Charlottenstraße 49, 10117 Berlin, tel: 20 33 8, fax: 20 33 61 69, <www.regenthotels.com>.* Sumptuously decorated hotel in the historic heart of Berlin, directly across from the Gendarmenmarkt. The service is exceptionally good. 195 rooms.

Hotel de Rome €€€€, *Behrenstraße 37, 10117 Berlin, tel: 460 60 90, fax: 460 60 92000, <www.roccofortehotels.com>.* This luxury hotel on Bebelplatz, next to the Staatsoper Unter den Linden, is located in a building which dates from 1889 and which housed the head office of Dresdner Bank until 1945. The ornate and classical design of the bank has been given a contemporary twist. 146 large bedrooms and suites. The bank vault is now a 20-metre (66-ft) swimming pool surrounded by a spa. The restaurant looks onto a large external terrace and offers alfresco dining during the summer.

Hotel Transit Loft €–€€ *Greifswalder Straße 219, 10405 Berlin-Prenzlauer Berg, tel: 484 937 73, fax: 440 510 74, <www.hotel-transit.de>.* Modern hotel in a converted 19th-century factory. The rooms (1–5 beds) are bright and functionally furnished, ideal for families with children and groups. All are en-suite, equipped with a shower and toilet. 47 rooms.

The Westin Grand Berlin €€€€ *Friedrichstraße 158–64, Berlin 10117, tel: 202 70, fax: 20 27 33 62, <http://aktuelles.westin.de/*

berlin>. This elegantly decorated, luxurious hotel at the corner of Friedrichstraße and Unter den Linden has excellent restaurants, a beautiful garden and top spa services. 358 rooms.

OUTSKIRTS

Hotel Maison Apartments am Kolk €€ *Kolk 10, 13597 Berlin, tel: 841 139 10, fax: 841 139 11, <www.aparthotel-amkolk.de>.* Eight charming furnished apartments with wireless internet in the medieval residential neighbourhood of Spandau *(see box page 81)*, with a weekly market and beer gardens overlooking the river Havel nearby. A short walk from the subway that takes you to central Berlin in just 20 minutes. Better suited for longer stays since there is an end-of-stay cleaning charge.

Schlosshotel im Grunewald €€€€ *Brahmsstraße 10, 14193 Berlin, tel: 895 84 0, fax: 895 84 800, <www.schlosshotelberlin.com>.* Luxurious elegance in an historic mansion set in a private park, with interior design by the illustrious Karl Lagerfeld. It has excellent leisure facilities, including sauna, solarium and swimming pool. Excellent restaurant. 54 rooms. During the FIFA World Cup the hotel was the home of the German national football team.

POTSDAM

art'otel Potsdam €€ *Zeppelinstraße 136, 14471 Potsdam, tel: (0331) 98 15 0, fax: (0331) 98 15 555, <www.artotel-potsdam.com>.* A stunning hotel situated on the banks of the Havel river. The building is a combination of a beautifully restored 19th-century granary and some striking modern architecture. Facilities include wireless internet connection, and a sauna, solarium and fitness area. 123 rooms.

Schlosshotel Cecilienhof €€€–€€€€ *Neuer Garten, 14469 Potsdam, tel: (0331) 3 70 50, fax: (0331) 29 24 98, <www.relexa hotels.de>.* English-style half-timbered country house built for the Kaiser's son, Crown Prince Wilhelm, this unique establishment is linked to the centre of Potsdam by bus or lovely lakeside footpath. A favourite with visiting heads of state. 42 rooms.

Recommended Restaurants

With scores of restaurants to choose from in Berlin, where do you start? To give you some guidance, we have made a selection covering a range of locations, types of cuisine and prices. However, restaurants are continually changing, so we recommend that you listen to local advice, as no list can be completely up-to-date.

There are very few really low-cost eating establishments in the city, although you will find several bargain pizza, pasta and burger places. Look for set menus, which are offered by most restaurants – they usually represent good value for money. As a basic guide, we have used the following symbols to give an idea of the price for a three-course meal for one, including a service charge of 15 percent, but excluding wine (drinks, especially wine, will add considerably to the final bill):

€€€	above €50
€€	€30–50
€	below €30

Many Berlin restaurants close for one or two days a week, around Christmas and New Year, and for a few weeks in summer. It's advisable to phone in advance, to make sure the restaurant is open.

BERLIN

BERLIN CITY, WEST

Diekmann €€€ *Meinekestraße 7, tel: 883 33 21.* This restaurant's interior looks like an old-fashioned store. The German-French style dishes are cooked with ingredients fresh from Brandenburg's fields, woods and waters. Open Monday–Saturday from noon, Sunday and holidays 6pm–1am.

First Floor €€€ *Budapester Straße 45, tel: 25 02 10 20.* International cuisine with the addition of German and French influences is served in this elegant restaurant in the Hotel Palace. Open noon–3pm and 6pm–1am Monday–Friday and 6pm–1am Saturday. Major credit cards.

Florian €€ *Grolmanstraße 52, tel: 313 91 84*. Noisy, intellectual chic in the fashionable area around Savignyplatz. Reservations advised. Open 6pm–3am daily. No credit cards.

Istanbul €–€€ *Pestalozzistraße 84, tel: 883 27 77*. Extensive menu offering a choice of delicious Turkish dishes, including vegetarian starters. Belly dancing on Friday and Saturday nights. Open daily noon–midnight. Major credit cards.

Kashmir Palace €€€ *Marburger Straße 14, tel: 214 28 40*. Sumptuous northern Indian food in an opulent setting. Open noon–3pm and 6pm–midnight daily. Major credit cards.

Kempinski-Grill €€€ *Kurfürstendamm 27, tel: 88 43 40*. Luxurious restaurant inside the Bristol-Kempinski Hotel *(see page 129)*. Alternatively, try the more informal Reinhard's, which serves regional specialities and has a lovely terrace. Open Tuesday–Sunday 1–3pm and 6pm– midnight, Monday 5pm–midnight. Major credit cards.

Leibniz-Klause €–€€ *Leibnizstraße 46, tel: 323 70 68*. Sophisticated and atmospheric pub-cum-restaurant with a tempting range of local and international dishes. Open noon–1am.

Lutter & Wegner €€ *Schlüterstraße 55, tel: 881 34 40*. An elegant Berlin institution which has been going strong since 1811. Jazz adds to the charm. Open daily 6pm–3am. Major credit cards.

Restaurant 44 €€€ *Augsburger Straße 44, at Swissôtel Berlin, tel: 220 10 22 88*. Enjoy creative and innovative cuisine in this stylish restaurant with a terrace overlooking the Ku'damm. Tim Raue, Guide GaultMillau's Chef of the Year 2007, and his team are proud to run one of the few Michelin-starred restaurants in Berlin. The menu features extravagant dishes that correspond with Tim Raue's culinary philosophy of tradition (regional cuisine) and evolution (avant-garde cuisine). Reservations necessary.

Wintergarten € *Fasanenstraße 23, tel: 882 54 14.* This haven of peace is situated in the Literaturhaus villa and is the perfect place to collect your thoughts after visiting the Käthe-Kollwitz Museum nearby. The salon at the back is ideal on sunny days. Open from 9.30am until 1am. No credit cards.

CHARLOTTENBURG

Alt Luxemburg €€€ *Windscheidstraße 31, tel: 323 87 30.* Excellent cuisine with a French touch, served in a tasteful ambiance. Reservations are strongly advised. Open Monday–Saturday from 5pm–1am. Major credit cards.

Don Quijote €€ *Bleibtreustraße 41, tel: 881 32 08.* This lively, long-established Spanish restaurant is notable for its excellent food, and has a friendly atmosphere. Open 4pm–1am daily. No credit cards.

Eiffel €€ *Ku'damm 105, tel: 891 13 05.* As the name implies, this is a French restaurant, though definitely with a Mediterranean touch. Much use has been made of wood and steel in the sleek interior. Open daily 9am–2am. Major credit cards.

La Sepia €€ *Marburger Straße 2, tel: 213 55 85.* This cosy Portuguese restaurant specialises in fish dishes, mainly grilled. Has a great, friendly atmosphere. Open noon–midnight Sunday–Thursday and noon–1am Friday and Saturday. No American Express or Diners Club.

Marjellchen €–€€ *Mommsenstraße 9, tel: 883 26 76.* Intimate, welcoming establishment specialising in unusual dishes from Germany's former eastern provinces, East and West Prussia, Pomerania and Silesia. Open 5pm–midnight. Closed Sunday.

Paris-Bar €€ *Kantstraße 152, tel: 313 80 52.* Classic French and international cuisine in intellectual/arty atmosphere. Popular meeting place for the young and seriously trendy. Open noon–2am daily. Major credit cards.

KREUZBERG

Henne € *Leuschnerdamm 25, tel: 614 77 30.* Not that keen on chicken? Then you haven't tried the *Milchmasthähnchen* (milk-fed chicken) here, almost the only fare on the menu. People flock to this unpretentious old Berlin *Wirtshaus* for it. Reserve in advance. Open Tuesday–Sunday 7pm–1am.

Hostaria del Monte Croce €€ *Mittenwalder Straße 6, tel: 694 39 68.* Copious portions of genuine Italian food in an authentic atmosphere in this tiny restaurant. Reserve in advance. Open for dinner only, from 7pm. Closed Sunday and Monday. Credit cards not accepted.

Liebermanns €€ *Lindenstr. 9-14, tel: 25 93 97 60.* The restaurant in the Jüdisches Museum is more than a museum café. Dishes are 'kosherstyle', which in this case means a young and creative Jewish cuisine. A popular highlight is the oriental buffet, accompanied by klezmer music live each Monday evening. Open Monday noon–10pm, Tuesday–Sunday noon–8pm.

Osteria No. 1 € *Kreuzbergstr. 71, tel: 782 91 62.* A lively ambience combined with delicious trattoria fare keep the regular young crowd flocking back for more. Reservations are highly recommended. Open daily noon–2am. American Express and Visa only.

MITTE

Berliner Republik und Brokers Bierbörse € *Schiffbauerdamm 8, tel: 30 87 22 93.* Big and breezy beer hall on the banks of the River Spree. As well as a good choice of solidly unpretentious food, there is an amazing range of beers, the prices of which go up and down on a screen as the demand for individual brews fluctuates from one moment to the next. Open 11.30am–4am. No credit cards.

Borchardt €€€ *Französische Straße 47, tel: 81 88 62 62.* An elegant, airy restaurant with a twenties atmosphere, conveniently situated just off the historic Gendarmenmarkt. The menu changes daily and portions are generous. Open daily 11.30am–1am. Major credit cards.

Brechts €€ *Schiffbauerdamm 6–7, tel: 28 59 85 85*. Where author Bertolt Brecht used to drink and dine. Located close to his theatre, the Berliner Ensemble, directly on the river Spree. Austrian and international cuisine of high quality is served.

Diekmann in Weinhaus Huth €€ *Alte Potsdamer Straße 5, tel: 25 29 75 24*. Supremely elegant French restaurant offering excellent value for money in the revitalised Potsdamer Platz. Open noon–1am daily. No Diners Club.

Dressler €€ *Unter den Linden 39, tel: 204 44 22*. Art deco style abounds in this sophisticated establishment which is styled on the great restaurants of the 1920s. International cuisine. There is also a sister restaurant, by the same name, at Ku'damm 207–208 (tel: 883 35 30). Both are open daily from 8am–1am. Major credit cards.

OpernPalais €–€€€ *Unter den Linden 5, tel: 20 26 83*. A popular dining centre in the heart of historic Berlin, just next to the Staatsoper, Operncafé is known for its lavish breakfast buffet, a selection of simple salads and a superlative choice of cakes. There are also musical shows at night. The Schinkel-Klause in the same complex offers traditional German fare in atmospheric cellar rooms. And there's one of the best outdoor terraces in Berlin. Open from 9am until midnight daily. Major credit cards.

Reinhard's €€ *Poststraße 28, tel: 242 52 95*. In the renovated Nikolaiviertel, this lively bistro, decorated in 1920s style, serves stylish cuisine to a mainly business clientele. Open daily from 9am until 1am. Major credit cards.

Rikes Gasthaus €–€€ *Potsdamer Straße 67, tel: 26 06 70*. Traditional Berlin dishes served in a cosy atmosphere in the Hotel Alt-Berlin. Open Monday–Saturday 5–11pm.

Ständige Vertretung € *Schiffbauerdamm 8, tel: 282 39 65.* Next door to the Berliner Republik, this cheerful establishment has an intriguing political theme, with photos, posters and much else decorating the walls. Serving typical Rhineland dishes and hoppy *kölsch* beer from Cologne, it's a welcoming home from home for politicians and civil servants exiled from the former seat of government in Bonn.

Unsicht-Bar Berlin €€–€€€ *Gormann Straße 14, tel: 24 34 25 00.* The food here is served in complete darkness by blind waiting staff. The idea is that removing sight gives your other senses – including taste – the chance to take over.

Vau €€€ *Jägerstraße 54–55, tel: 20 29 730.* Elegant, unpretentious establishment serving outstanding northern German and international cuisine. The service is friendly, and there is a small courtyard for pleasant lunches outside in the summer. Open Monday–Saturday noon–2.30pm and 7–10.30pm. Credit cards except Mastercard.

Zur Letzten Instanz €€ *Waisenstraße 14–16, tel: 242 55 28.* Berlin's oldest restaurant, founded in 1621, serves delicious regional cuisine and offers great set menus or buffets for travel groups.

FURTHER AFIELD

Blockhaus Nikolskoe €€ *Nikolskoer Weg, Wannsee, tel: 805 29 14.* Classic German cuisine in an old dacha originally built for Tsar Nicholas I, in a lovely setting overlooking the Havel and Peacock Island. Open 10am–10pm April–October and 10am–7pm November–April. Visa only.

Café Einstein € *Kurfürstenstraße 58, tel: 261 50 96.* This Viennese-style coffeehouse provides international newspapers which you can read in a delightfully literary ambience while enjoying the outstanding selection of delicious cakes. There is also a branch in Unter den Linden. Open 10am–2am daily. No credit cards.

Candela € *Grunewaldstraße 81, tel: 782 14 09.* Pizza and pasta are the staples of this lively restaurant, which combines Italian and

French cuisine. It also offers a changing day menu. Food is authentic and the service is good. Open daily from 5pm–1am. Visa only.

Forsthaus Paulsborn €€–€€€ *Hüttenweg 90, Grunewald, tel: 818 19 10.* An attractive restaurant in a hunting lodge in the heart of the forest, with a fine selection of game dishes as well as smoked Scottish salmon. Reservations advisable. Open in winter 11am–6pm, in summer from 11am–11pm, Tuesday–Sunday; closed Monday. Major credit cards.

Nola €€ *Dortmunder Straße 9, tel: 399 69 69.* A rising star among Berlin restaurants, this serves California-style food in a lively, sophisticated atmosphere. Excellent cocktails and a great place to watch beautiful people. Open 4pm–1am Monday–Saturday and 10am–1am Sunday. Dinner served until 11.30pm. Major credit cards.

Offenbachstuben €€ *Stubbenkammerstraße 8, tel: 445 85 02.* Charming restaurant which was renowned during the GDR years. Each of the four little rooms is beautifully decorated, and there are entrancing touches, such as the still-working 100-year-old ballet machine. Excellent German-French food. Open 6pm–1am daily. Major credit cards.

Pasternak € *Knaackstraße 22–24, tel: 441 33 99.* In the trendy borough of Prenzlauer Berg, this restaurant serves typical Russian food to a clientele of artists and intellectuals revelling in its authentic atmosphere. Open daily 10am–2am. No credit cards.

Restauration 1900 €€ *Husemannstraße 1, tel: 442 24 94.* International cuisine predominates in this select restaurant in the heart of Prenzlauer Berg which, like Offenbachstuben *(see above)*, was a favourite even before the Wall came down. Good vegetarian selection. The wine list is good and the service attentive. Reservations essential. Open 9am–1am daily. Major credit cards.

Udagawa €€ *Feuerbachstraße 24, Steglitz, tel: 792 23 73.* Excellent Japanese cuisine. Reservations essential. Open 5.30–11.30pm daily (except Tuesday). Major credit cards.

INDEX

Berlitz pocket guide

Berlin

Ninth Edition 2008
Reprinted 2009

Written by Brigitte Lee, Jack Messenger
and Jack Altman
Revised by Mike Ivory
Updated by Ortrun Egelkraut
Series Editor: Tony Halliday

Printed in Singapore by Insight Print
Services (Pte) Ltd, 38 Joo Koon Road,
Singapore 628990. Tel: (65) 6865-1600.
Fax: (65) 6861-6438

Berlitz Trademark Reg. U.S. Patent Office
and other countries. Marca Registrada

Every effort has been made to provide
accurate information in this publication,
but changes are inevitable. The publisher
cannot be responsible for any resulting
loss, inconvenience or injury.

Contact us

At Berlitz we strive to keep our guides as
accurate and up to date as possible, but if you
find anything that has changed, or if you have
any suggestions on ways to improve this guide,
then we would be delighted to hear from you.

Berlitz Publishing, PO Box 7910,
London SE1 1WE, England.
fax: (44) 20 7403 0290
email: berlitz@apaguide.co.uk
www.berlitzpublishing.com